THE NEW NATO
Its Survival and Resilience

Mohammed Moustafa Orfy

authorHOUSE®

AuthorHouse™ UK Ltd.
500 Avebury Boulevard
Central Milton Keynes, MK9 2BE
www.authorhouse.co.uk
Phone: 08001974150

First published by AuthorHouse 9/24/2007

ISBN: 978-1-4343-3564-7 (sc)

Printed in the United States of America
Bloomington, Indiana

This book is printed on acid-free paper.

To my family…

TABLE OF CONTENTS

PREFACE

This brief book is intended to review and focus upon the evolution of the North Atlantic Alliance from the end of the Cold War to the present day. The aim is to increase and enhance understanding of, and assess the predictability of, the nature, extent, and limits of the Alliance's strategy in the coming decades. To reach this end, the following four questions will be explored in detail.

A) Why has the Alliance survived despite the ending of the Cold War and the reason for its existence having been eliminated?

B) What are the main factors, aspects and impacts of its huge transformation process?

C) What is the new or current rationale behind, or the raison d'être of, its continuity at present?

D) What is the future of the Alliance in the light of the emerging, perhaps growing, rift between the United States and Europe?

CHAPTER ONE
NATO IN THE POST-COLD WAR WORLD

The sudden collapse of the former Soviet Union meant the disappearance of the external enemy that had made the existence of the North Atlantic Alliance totally indispensable for the safety and security of the West for more than four decades. The end of the enormous Soviet threat and the subsequent dismantling of the Warsaw pact, literally the raison d'être of NATO, occurred in a manner that had been neither envisaged nor expected. The resulting situation raised some questions about the continuing need for the Alliance in the post Cold War world or indeed the feasibility of keeping it alive. These open–ended and unanswered questions quickly turned out to be doubts and uncertainties to the extent that led some notable observers and commentators to consider that NATO could be the only victim of its own overwhelming victory in the Cold War. To give an example, Calleo (1987:215) indicates that 'the Alliance grows less and less viable in its present form, but a viable alternative seems possible'.

History is an ongoing source of knowledge, but historical events are not necessarily repeatable. Although the experience of history might suggest that Alliances which have already fulfilled the needs and objectives of the allies in a particular set of circumstances will lose the coherence that held member states together and subsequently dissolve, the case of the North Atlantic Alliance is unique. There appears to be no point of comparison between the most successful Alliance in recent history and Alliances from other epochs; therefore, history seems unable to provide the necessary clarification in this context.

Given the lack of historical parallels, it might be useful to refer to theoretical interpretations. In fact, the continuity of the Alliance could be understood in the light of different theories, including organizational, institutional, and system. To start with, McCalla (2002:457) argues that:

> "Organizational" literature makes it clear that organizations and their members engage in three general types of behavior to ensure continuity and survival: resistance to change, affirmation of organizational necessity, and adaptation.

Following this framework, Kourvetaris (2002) states:

> From the organizational perspective, we can draw a number of inferences regarding NATO's continuity and persistence. These are:
> a) NATO members are not willing to dismantle the organization;
> b) NATO members have reaffirmed the value of the Alliance;
> c) NATO has modified its original role and missions to adapt to new realities and generate new missions.

In line with the 'system' theory, it could be noted that NATO is not only a military organization but also has all the characteristics of an open and strong system. The member states share well-defined systems of values, norms, aims and perceptions. Some theorists hold the view that the concepts of morphostasis (the process that helps the system to maintain itself) and morphogenesis (the process that helps the system change) are also integral parts of the Alliance's system. As a normal consequence, the Alliance's internal or built-in ability for adaptation has paved the way towards its survival; by virtue of displaying the interactions between both processes: morphostasis and morphogenesis.

From another perspective, McCalla (2002:465) cogently summarizes the international 'institutionalist' approach of NATO members as follows:

a) NATO members utilize existing norms and procedures within NATO to deal with new problems instead of creating new ones;

b) Member states are willing to modify cuts and downsizing to deal with problems;

c) NATO members use the regime as the basis for ties to other actors, states, and non-states in pursuit of regime goals.

From another perspective, two schools of thought could be more helpful in explaining the reasons for the emergence of Alliances and their continuity. Firstly, the idealistic perspective suggests that nations commit themselves to fight alongside each other because of the shared values and ideas, which deserve to be protected and defended. For example, at the latest NATO Summit, Riga 28-29 November 2006, the heads of state and governments of the member countries reaffirmed, in paragraph 1, that:

Our resolve to meet the security challenges of the 21stcentury and defend our populations and common values, while maintaining a strong collective defence as the core purpose of our Alliance; Our 26 nations are united in democracy, individual liberty and the rule of law, and faithful to the purposes and principles of the United Nations Charter'.

They added in Paragraph 3 that:

> From Afghanistan to the Balkans and from the Mediterranean Sea to Darfur, in six challenging missions and operations in three geographic regions, we are advancing peace and security and standing shoulder-to-shoulder with those who defend our common values of democracy and freedom as embodied in the Washington Treaty.

Secondly, the realistic perspective ascribes the necessity of the existence of the Alliances to logic and the analysis of costs and benefits. This means that Alliances can normally protect interests and multiply benefits through the division of responsibilities and labour; and their existence as such, over and above this, may deter any standing hostilities. For instance, the Riga Summit declaration states, in Paragraph 2, that:

> The principle of the indivisibility of Allied security is fundamental, and our solidarity gives us the strength to meet new challenges together. In today's evolving security environment, we confront complex, sometimes inter-related threats such as terrorism, increasingly global in scale and lethal in results, and the proliferation of Weapons of Mass Destruction and their means of delivery, as well as challenges from instability due to failed or failing states. This puts a premium on the vital role NATO plays as the essential forum for security consultation between North American and European Allies.

In general, these two perspectives could be valid for the case of the North Atlantic Alliance and its continuity in the post Cold War era. On the one hand, it would be possible to justify the survival of the Alliance so far by indicating that the allies share the same values, such as democracy, the rule of law and respect for human rights. On the other hand, it could be argued that there is still a vital interest for them in supporting the spread of their values worldwide, either for the sake of humanity or even in the context of security calculations. Meanwhile, others may raise the argument that the allies are still in need of each other, in terms of the cost and benefits, to defend themselves better in such a dangerous and uncertain world.

Apart from this theoretical explanation, it is clear that there were some practical and persuasive reasons that pushed the allies not only to agree to preserve their Alliance, but also to embark on a huge and continuous transformation process in order to adapt their Alliance to the new realities and different determinates of the new global geo-strategic environment.

For the sake of brevity, it seems sufficient to note that the ambiguity and chaos which characterized the beginning of the post Cold War era made the Alliance itself more a matter of asset, and less of liability. In other words, the member states, rapidly and wisely enough, recognized that the historic changes which had simultaneously occurred in the international arena made the world even more dangerous than before; as increasing, uncontrollable and asymmetric threats emerged out of the blue.

In fact, many circumstances have rendered the world more dangerous. These include: the outbreak of ethnic, religious and tribal violence; the disappearance of states or what might be called the phenomenon of the failing states; the increasing scarcity of natural resources; the exacerbation of the international economic and social situation; the negative consequences of globalization; the proliferation of weapons of mass destruction alongside the availability of the accompanying technology and means of delivery; and the rise of fundamentalism, which has replaced the previous ideological conflicts.

But, how and why did this happen? The answer would seem to lie in the fact that the end of the mutual fear between the two main superpowers and their subordinates, which grew out of the nuclear deterrent, has encouraged many groups worldwide to take advantage of the new global scene to try to restore or defend what they consider to be their legal, looted, or hereditary rights. Suffice it to refer to the case of the fragmentation of former Yugoslavia, something which caused a huge human catastrophe for millions of people in the heart of Europe. Another example is the case of Rwanda, in which about one million people were slaughtered in tribal and ethnic violence in only a matter of weeks. Moreover, the globalization process, as explained before, has had negative effects on world security.

Such alarming developments convinced the United States and other member states, unequivocally and irrevocably, that nothing could prevent the spilling over of these uncontrollable events into their areas of interest. Consequently, there was a vital interest not only in keeping the Alliance workable, but also in changing its nature, structure, and strategic concept. In short, the allies perceived that the absence of the Alliance could jeopardize the allies' security and thereby necessitate huge and swift changes to their defence and security policies, which would have been, for the majority of them, unaffordable. Gebhard (1994:6) notes that 'the marginal cost of maintenance will invariably be less than attempting to rebuild Alliances in times of crisis'.

Furthermore NATO, as such, has been a leitmotif of the prestigious US position worldwide, as well as the main vehicle of US influence on the European continent. It remains the only organization that constantly brings together the United States and European allies to consult and co-operate on various security and political matters. Undeniably, the United States has enjoyed, since NATO's establishment in 1949, the most prestigious position in the Alliance. This is not only because of its nuclear military capability, which has served as an umbrella for Europe against any nuclear attacks since the long decades of the Cold War till now, but also its more advanced conventional military strength, which has a far higher capability than that of the European allies. Over and above this, the United States has borne the biggest share of the Alliance's budget from NATO's beginning until the present time. Perceivably, foregoing such a position in this long and well-established organization could allow some countries of the 'old Europe' to play the kind of role that would or could collide with the United States' interests in certain areas. Sadakata (2003) maintians that:

> Generally speaking, the US administrations have understood international organization as follows; they could help the US to spread burdens, control risks, and promote its values; they could also legitimize and universalize its interests at a time when it needed to reassure others about the way it would use its pre-dominant position in the global system.

Put simply, as long as the United States believes that NATO's existence serves these goals, it will strive to preserve it in the future, unless there is a US policy change in this regard, which is a very remote probability.

In addition, although the possibility of a clash between great powers in the post Cold War order, sometimes and perhaps correctly described as the world of disorder, seems to be a slim one, it can not be ruled out totally. Shen (2004) observes that:

> Realistically, governments have been competing and hedging against one another since the seventeenth century, and until the international stage is truly transformed into a new world order in which trust and co-operation prevail, there is no reason to believe that states will abandon the technique of creating various groupings, such as Alliances, to help ensure their national security.

Practically speaking, NATO has been the only multilateral institution in which the allies have confidence or trust because its capabilities are so strong and effective that they could be used at any time against a range of serious threats. The possibility of major war is somehow unrealistic, but states are likely to prepare themselves for the worst possible scenarios. Russia, for example, has been passing through a transitional period. Nothing could guarantee that the ultra-nationalist movement will not be able to seize power in the future. Furthermore, historical evidence suggests that the emerging boom in military and economic capabilities in China could induce the Chinese ruling elite to challenge US global hegemony, bearing in mind that the two poles have contradicting and conflicting views about the future of Taiwan.

Importantly, and perhaps interestingly, some adopt the view that the Alliance has been trying to create a long-standing enemy to preserve its coherence and interests. For example, the ex-Secretary General, W.Claes, selected Islam or the Islamic world, numbering almost 54 countries, as the most dangerous and conclusive source of threat to the interests of the West following the disappearance of the Soviet threat. Although, this claim or vision did not exceed the limits of discussions between intellectuals in media circles or think tanks, it may give an indication of the way of thinking of one of the most important and influential figures to participate in drawing up the strategy lines of the Western world in the post Cold War era.

In addition, NATO has created, throughout the past five decades, a large civilian and military bureaucracy. It also has a very big lobby, in almost every related field: professional and academic circles, thinks tanks, and the press, which derives benefits and importance from the Alliance. Experience and history also indicate that large institutions do not die easily. Their defendants, who are normally more organized, oppose any attempt at dismantling or lowering the level of usability of these institutions for their own good. Meanwhile, opponents or sceptics may ultimately get crippled because of the lukewarm response of others or uncertainty about the prospects of success.

Finally, the United States and the European allies have held onto the vision that the new transformed NATO would help in creating a safer West by encouraging every democratic European state to join. The main purpose or theme of the transformation process was, and still is, to put an end to Stalin's artificial division of Europe forever. What is to be borne in mind, at this point, is that admitting or annexing new members implies that the new members must have undertaken to adopt Western values, such as democracy and human rights, and to adapt their policies as well as structures in accordance with NATO's criteria and requirements.

Chernoff (1995:261) identifies certain factors that rule out the possibility of dismantling the Alliance, including the following:

> The members of NATO as shown, have an incentive to continue
> to co-operate on political and security questions because they
> have: (i) past experience of successful co-operation with one

another, (ii) shared desires for fiscal saving that arms control and defense co-operation provoke, (iii) common economic interests, and (iv) similar social and cultural values; in addition (v) the small western European states, without the Alliance would become more vulnerable to a variety of dangers.

Duignan (2000:82-119) argues that 'the end of the Cold War did not mean, as some claimed or predicted, that NATO had lost its reason for being'. He notes that 'NATO was, factually, formed to keep the Russians out, the Germans down, and the Americans involved in Europe, ' and predicts that 'in the future, terrorism and biological, chemical, and nuclear warfare will all have to be dealt with by NATO, besides facing challenges in the Middle East and in the Gulf, etc'. Moreover, Kay (2003:20) expresses the conviction that overall, the current duties of the Alliance remain unchanged including:

> Providing further U.S involvement in Euro-Atlantic relations, mitigating historical animosity between certain European allies, integrating East European states and Russia in Euro-Atlantic area.

In brief, the reasons for maintaining the Alliance have not completely disappeared; on the contrary, new factors have emerged which have underpinned the importance and vitality of the Alliance. It is noteworthy that the discussions on the feasibility or vitality of NATO were, at the outset, strong and fierce, but have become less strident in the light of the above-mentioned factors.

CHAPTER TWO

THE TRANSFORMATION PROCESS OF NATO

It would be prudent now to highlight that all the previously explained determinates have granted the necessary momentum for the unprecedented and continuous transformation process. Remarkably, the member states began the transformation process of the Alliance even before the demise of the former Soviet Union, and are still working on it at this moment. This ongoing and far-reaching policy has profoundly transformed NATO from a Cold War collective security organization into a new organization. As such, it takes a comprehensive and holistic approach to dealing with all pressing security issues, by attaching more importance to the political dimension. Fundamentally, this new approach has included the expansion of the area of interest or geographical focus beyond NATO's traditional territory. The following analysis will evaluate the major trends of the transformation process.

(I) - The 1991 Strategic Concept

As the Alliance started its transformation process, it was necessary and unavoidable to change the guiding principles. Consequently, at a meeting of the North Atlantic Council in Rome 1991, the heads of state and government, while reaffirming the basic principles and concepts of the Alliance, approved and adopted the first ever published Strategic Concept. The remarkable and momentous effects of this strategic concept could be illustrated as follows:

A) The Alliance is purely defensive in purpose; and NATO's policy is based on the collective defence and indivisibility of the security of the allies. Previously, the allies reassured, at the London summit 1990, the former Soviet Union saying that:

> We will remain a defensive Alliance and will continue to defend all the territory of all our members ......, we have no aggressive intention ... we will never in any circumstances be the first to use force.

B) For the first time, the Alliance started to define and recognize security calculations, not specifically in terms of the traditional massive confrontation, but rather from a multi-faceted perspective. Paragraphs 5, 8 and 9 stated that:

> The monolithic, massive and potentially immediate threat which was the principal concern of the Alliance in its first forty years has disappeared; unlike the predominant threat of the past, the risks to allied security are multi-faceted in nature and multi-directional as well as hard to predict and assess; these risks are the result of the adverse consequences of instabilities that may arise from the serious economic, social and political difficulties, including ethnic rivalries and territorial despites, which are faced by many countries in Central and Eastern Europe.

Furthermore, Article 12 underlined the need to take into account that, 'the Alliance security interest can be affected by other risks of a wider nature, including proliferation of weapons of mass destruction, disruption of the flow of vital resources and actions of terrorism and sabotage'. This new thought appears to have amounted to a radical change in the Alliance's doctrine.

C) The fundamental tasks of the Alliance were clearly identified in certain directions. These included:

> The maintenance of a military capability sufficient to prevent war and to provide for effective defense, an overall capability to manage successfully crises affecting the security of its members, and the pursuit of political efforts favoring dialogue with other nations; as well as the active search for a co-operative approach to European security, including the field of arms control and disarmament.

Noticeably, more emphasis was increasingly given to the political dimension with regard to achieving the goals of the security policy in general. In the same context, the heads of state and government participating in a London summit, in 1990, stated that:

> We reaffirm that security and stability do not lie solely in the military dimension, and we intend to enhance the political component of our Alliance as provided for by Article 2 of our treaty. (Para 2).

D) The importance of the Middle Eastern and South Mediterranean regions started to emerge in the strategic calculations of the Alliance. Seemingly, the alleviation of NATO's worry towards the arsenal of the

'Soviet Union, both conventional and nuclear' enabled the Alliance to speed up its steps in the transformation process and turn its eyes towards the security matters on its southern periphery. The Strategic Concept assured that the stability and peace of the countries on the southern periphery of Europe were important for the security of the Alliance, 'as was noticeable during the 1991 Gulf war'. This concern could be observed in certain paragraphs, especially Paragraph 11 which stated, 'The allies also wish to maintain peaceful and non adversarial relations with the countries of the southern Mediterranean and Middle East'. This importance was accompanied by reference to the build–up of military power and the proliferation of weapons' technologies in the area, including weapons of mass destruction and ballistic missiles capable of reaching the territory of some member states. It could be understood that the experience gained from the first Gulf War over-shadowed the Alliance's assessment at that time. In fact, the priority currently being given to the Middle East could be traced back to that time, bearing in mind that it was strongly believed that all global threats against the interests of the Alliance, as identified by article 12, existed, and still do, in the turbulent Middle Eastern region. At that time, there was no big focus upon the danger of fundamentalism or terrorism. As will be shown later, terrorism has become one of the main concerns of the Alliance and almost synonymous with Middle Eastern issues.

E) It was confirmed that the new world environment did not change the purpose or the security functions of the Alliance. While emphasizing the enduring vitality of the Alliance, the document underlined certain themes: the need to adopt a broader approach to security (Para 14); the scope of the Alliance, as well as member states' rights and obligations as provided for in the Washington treaty, remained unchanged (Para 22); there was a unique opportunity to change the structure, size and readiness of forces accordingly and maintain for the foreseeable future an appropriate mix of nuclear and conventional forces, (part IV); the

Alliance would keep the necessary flexibility for further developments in the politico-military environment, with regard to new emerging risks.

F) The strategic concept also confirmed the Alliance's determination to pursue vigorously further progress in arms control and confidence-building measures. It should be noted that Paragraph 50 highlighted that:

> While the Alliance is not dependent on chemical warfare capability, it remains committed to the earliest possible achievement of a global, comprehensive and effectively verifiable ban of all chemical weapons.

Again, this may explain why the Middle East became, at that time, one of the top priorities for the Alliance.

G) The preferable and chosen working strategy for the Alliance was based on three factors, as was also declared in the 1991 Rome Declaration and its subsequent documents. This formula was expressed as follows:

> Our security policy can now be based on three mutually reinforcing elements: dialogue, co-operation, and the maintenance of a collective defense capability…and use, as appropriate, of these elements will be particularly important to prevent or manage the crisis.

H) The document showed prudence by, from the very beginning of the transformation process, excluding any idea of a possible clash between the NATO's role or purpose with the completion of European defence and security policy. None of the subsequent major documents ignored such an issue. Instead, there have been many statements confirming and assuring that there should and will be no overlapping of the work or collision of interests between the two different entities, and the importance of ensuring transparency and complementarity between them. Frequent confirmation was also made that a stronger unified European policy, in this respect, would add to the Alliance's ability and enable European allies to perform their role, eventually narrowing the capabilities gap between the two pillars, Europe and the United States.

In general, the first major step on the long road of the transformation process which was the 1991 Strategic Concept, resulted in some major trends. These trends have included: complete and radical change, by which the Alliance has become not only a military but also a security and political organization; change in the definition of security through which various sources of threats were identified; agreement on preserving the basic concepts, purposes, and tasks of the Alliance through showing both flexibility and adherence in order to fulfil the requirements of the adaptation process; and recognition of the need to deal with the danger coming from the south, as a repercussion of the first Gulf War.

These concepts guided the transformation process throughout the following years, and were repeatedly and frequently underpinned and underlined by the documents issued by different summits and ministerial meetings of the Alliance during the nineties.

(II) - The 1999 Strategic Concept

With the passing of years, the United States realised that the appropriate time had come to instigate a turning point in the history of the

Alliance in order to accelerate and boast its transformation process in an inclusive manner. Therefore, on NATO's 50th anniversary in April 1999, the member states gathered in Washington to review and assess the developments of the transformation process of the North Atlantic Alliance. The remarkable result of this historic summit was the issuance of the updated Strategic Concept, which was formulated to provide the necessary guidance for every detailed policy and strategy of the Alliance in the twenty-first century. The new concept, similar to the 1991 concept, addressed public opinion in an attempt to show good will and a sincere desire for co-operation with others in the light of the absence of confrontational attitudes and ideological conflicts.

Briefly, it reaffirmed the high importance of the transatlantic link between North America and Europe, and the indivisibility of their security and interests. Then it reviewed, contributed to and highlighted the new patterns of co-operation, such as partnership for peace, and dialogue, as well as some guiding polices, such as conflict prevention, crisis management, and arms control. In addition, it underlined the co-operative links with European security and defence policy. Likewise, the document granted the necessary guidance for the process of re-structuring the Alliance forces, and defined the new characteristics of conventional and nuclear forces. This broad-based approach reflected, in essence, the willingness of member states, mainly the United States, to pursue their efforts to push the Alliance forward in such a way as to give more 'added value' to their safety and security. Put another way, this summit raised the slogan that 'we the allies would enter the twenty first century together, armed by our transformed Alliance'.

It is extremely important to examine and review the basic points of this strategic concept in order to assess the evolution of the Alliance at the turn of the century, with a view to defining the determinates of its new global strategy in the coming decades. The assessment of the basic points could be shown as follows:

A– With respect to the security challenges, the strategic concept indicated that, although the danger of general war in Europe, or against the Alliance in general, has virtually disappeared, the other sources of danger to the interests of member states still exist. These dangers include ethnic conflict, the abuse or massive violation of human rights, political instability, economic fragility which may lead eventually to disastrous social conditions, the proliferation of weapons of mass destruction and their means of delivery, and the danger of terrorism. At this point, observation could also be made that the sources of danger, as identified in this updated document, as well as the 1991 document, were so diverse and huge that it became imperative to change or develop the scope, jurisdiction, and the area of interests of the Alliance. This dictated transforming the Alliance from a collective defence and security organization, strictly limited to the Euro-Atlantic area, to a global security organization which has to prepare itself to deter hostilities and deal with the spillover or ramifications of the various security threats.

B- The document reaffirmed the need to preserve a vivid and dynamic partnership between Europe and North America. As far as European policy is concerned, the updated strategic concept was decisive in affirming that the European security and defence identity would continue to be developed within the Alliance on the basis of the decision taken by Alliance foreign ministers in Berlin in 1996 and thereafter. The document stated that this process would require close co-operation between the two sides, and then affirmed that this process would enable the European allies to contribute in a more effective manner to the Alliance's activities and missions. Noticeably, the arrangements that were agreed upon, at that time, with respect to the determinates of the relationship between the Alliance and European security and defence identity asserted that: 'The European allies will be able to act on their own, by themselves, though, the readiness of the Alliance, on a case by case basis and by consensus'. In return, the Alliance would make its assets and capabilities available for European-led operations, in which NATO is not engaged militarily. Arguably, this sort of partnership, while it acknowledged the mutual needs of the two partners, implied, even dictated, that Europe must continue to be related to America, not move off in its own direction. The approved criteria have imposed the idea that any European movement whatsoever must follow NATO's choice as to whether to intervene or not, meaning in reality the United States has the calling.

C- In spite of the absence of the probability of any major attack, the concept confirmed the need to maintain effective and efficient military capabilities, which are adequate and appropriate to the existing security circumstances. These range from collective defence, the central theme of the Alliance's strategy, to crisis response operation. The expression 'crisis response operation' is, in fact, very flexible and can be extended to include different kinds of operations. Certainly, the Alliance, at that moment, seems to have realised the need to accelerate the process of changing the structure, size, nature and readiness of its forces. Definitely, the experience gained in Bosnia and Kosovo led the Alliance's strategic planners to recognize that the future military missions are likely to take place outside the member states' territories. They also realised that, most probably, these operations would involve a range of troops from both allied and non-allied partner countries; therefore, different skills and training were duly needed to carry out such operations in a successful manner. To achieve this objective, the Washington summit launched DCI, NATO Defense Capabilities Initiative, in order to prepare the Alliance's forces to deter hostilities in the twenty-first century. To elaborate further, the aim of DCI is to achieve certain objectives, which are mobility, deployability, sustainability, effective engagement, survivability and interoperable communications and surveillance. The Alliance's documents explained the following:

> Mobility and deployability means ability to deploy forces quickly where they are needed, even outside the area of Alliance; sustainability means ability to maintain and supply forces far from their home bases; effective engagement means the ability to successfully engage and fight an enemy or adversary in different types of operations; survivability means the ability to protect forces and infrastructure against any possible threats; interoperable communications means that compatible and successful command and control and information exchange mechanisms.

In addition, the need for improvement in surveillance and reconnaissance, in order to achieve the necessary protection of forces on out-of-area mission, was also recognised in this document.

The final and conclusive impact of the changes to the Alliance's forces, which were effected throughout the transformation process as a whole and DCI in particular, was a significant reduction in the size of forces and a tangible increase in mobility and readiness. For instance, some major developments took place from 1991 to 1997, such as defence budgets decreasing by 30 per cent; armed forces decreased in size by 28 to 40 per cent for most countries; land forces were down 25 per cent; major warships by 20 per cent; and combat aircraft by 30 per cent; US forces in Europe were down 66 per cent, from a total of 300, 000 to 100, 000 military personnel; air wings reduced from 4 to 2; and brigades from 17 to 4 since 1989; all chemical weapons were withdrawn; and eighty per cent of nuclear weapons were withdrawn; NATO's integrated command structure has been reduced or streamlined since 1990, etc. Recently, documents have disclosed that this trend has continued: for instance, ground forces have been cut by 25 per cent, major naval vessels by some 40 per cent and air force combat squadrons by some 40 per cent.

This nature of the change in the Alliance's forces appears to be irrefutable evidence of its seriousness in anticipating movement out of the Euro-Atlantic area, to defend the interests of member states whenever and wherever necessary, without ignoring the need to keep the minimum of military readiness capable of facing major events in its main area. This could be considered almost a complete shift in the Alliance's doctrine, transforming it from only a "defensive" to a 'defensive and offensive' organization, in nature, preparedness and orientation.

Seemingly, the Alliance has chosen to follow the advice of some observers and analysts who previously argued that NATO had to adopt an 'outward-looking strategy' and conduct 'out-of-area operations', otherwise it would be 'out of business'.

Importantly, the adherence shown to international legitimacy and the role of the United Nations, underlined by the 1999 Strategic Concept, set a legal limit for the future manœuvering of the Alliance, and seemed designed to alleviate the worries of others worldwide. In other words, mentioning the United Nations as a point of reference simply meant that NATO still, at that time, fully abided by international law, and was not seeking to obtain the right to identify when to strike other than by the will of the international community. Noticeably, assurance of this nature, addressed to others, tends to have disappeared from recent Alliance documents, especially with regard to terrorism; on the contrary, new arguments and pretexts have been repeatedly mentioned to justify the need for anticipated or even pre-emptive actions without waiting for international approval.

D-The document also paid great importance to the Alliance's prospective role with regard to conflict prevention and crisis management. Again, the concept of conflict prevention highlighted the political dimension of the Alliance. This political role, which may include the role of diplomacy and consultation etc, has been widening in recent years to the extent that has led NATO officials to frequently emphasize that NATO is a 'politico-security/military' organization, ignoring that NATO, by nature and structure, was mainly a military organization.

E-The document pointed out the principal instruments which the Alliance has been using in dealing with non-member states, especially those on its periphery. These instruments include the Partnership for Peace, the Euro-Atlantic Partnership Council, the special or distinctive relationships with both Russia and Ukraine, and the Mediterranean Dialogue. The declared notion that accompanied the launching of the whole process was that 'it would not exclude anybody' in participating in the efforts aimed at enhancing security and overcoming the roots of misperception, lack of trust, and division which may cause conflicts. Apparently, the importance given to the Middle East, was somehow confined to the South Mediterranean dialogue countries and did not amount to occupying the top priority of NATO's policy, as happened later in the post 9-11 period.

F-Finally, the strategic concept showed unlimited support for pursuing and exerting all efforts to realise the aims set out by the Alliance's policy, with regard to arms control, disarmament, and non proliferation. It also assured that this aspect of the Alliance's policy would be dealt with in harmony with its approach to defence, etc. The point was formulated as follows:

The strategy underlines the indispensable part that Alliance forces play in addressing the risks associated with the proliferation of nuclear, biological and chemical weapons and their means of delivery.

Thus, it might be argued that the strategic concept, while not stating detailed measures with regard to the above-mentioned aims, left a lot of room for interpretation of its intention in this regard, i.e. whether these aims will be achieved by forcible and coercive policies, or through voluntarily persuasive means. It seems that, at the Washington summit, concern about certain conventional weapons, like ballistic missiles, did not appear to be considered particularly important, which was not the case at subsequent Alliance summits.

Broadly speaking, one can conclude that the new strategic concept, as agreed upon at the 1999 Washington summit, was a classic compromise document that successfully sought to hide or shroud the existing differences in attitudes and policies between the allies in an ambiguous formula that could be interpreted in different manners afterwards. Clearly, the document bridged the gap between the need to develop the role of the Alliance and a keenness to respect the principles of international law. This balance was achieved through what could be described as language of 'constructive ambiguity', the kind which could normally satisfy the different attitudes of the allies.

In fact, the two previously evaluated strategic concepts laid down and paved the way for launching certain mechanisms which constitute the backbone of the Alliance's transformation process. The following review will focus upon some of those mechanisms with the aim of identifying the basic dynamics and factors of the change process, i.e. from a regional to global organization. This will also help to make predictions about the Alliance's continuity as well as the various dimensions of its strategy in future.

(III) -The enlargement

Fundamentally, the most important feature of the transformation process has been the enlargement mechanism by which every democratic European country has the right to seek to join the Alliance by following the appropriate preparatory procedures. This has come about in conformity with Article 10, of the 1949 North Atlantic Treaty, in which the allies clearly stated and undertook that: The parties may, by unanimous agreement, invite any other European state in a position to further the principles of this treaty and to contribute to the security of the North Atlantic area to accede to this treaty.

This process started even before the end of the Cold War for different political and strategic calculations, so that the numbers of signatories of the treaty increased from 12 to 16 states.

With the end of the Cold War and the beginning of the continued transformation process, the Alliance has repeated again that this enlargement process would not exclude any country that is able to fulfil the requirements of membership. On the other hand, the frequently-mentioned notion was that this enlargement would not threaten anybody; as the Alliance would remain, definitely, a defensive Alliance. The Czech Republic, Hungary and Poland were the first ones to join the Alliance in 1999; and this move embodied the first serious application of the enlargement process. Of course, these countries rushed to seek membership because of the fear of falling again into the sphere of influence of the Russian nation in future. Symbolically, the joining of the former Warsaw Pact countries confirmed and crystallized the seriousness of the transformation process, and the full adherence given to it by member states of the Alliance.

The second major round of the enlargement process took place a few years later. At the Prague Summit, 2002, the Heads of State and Government issued invitations to seven countries to begin accession talks to join the Alliance. These were Bulgaria, Estonia, Latvia, Lithuania, Romania, Slovakia and Slovenia. On 29 March 2004, these seven countries formally joined the Alliance. This was the fifth and biggest round of enlargement in the Alliance's history. The successful and peaceful way in which these countries, especially Latvia, joined the Alliance constitutes uncontested proof of the success and wisdom of the Alliance's policy with regard to achieving the two main aims: the first is admitting the countries of strategic importance; the second is to achieve this enlargement without igniting Russian worries.

Currently, three candidate countries: Albania, Croatia and the Former Yugoslav Republic of Macedonia – are preparing themselves to join the Alliance through their participation in NATO's 'Membership Action Plan'. This (MAP) was designed to assist and prepare partner countries to meet NATO's standards in order to obtain membership in the near future. It is noteworthy that the applicant countries must not be involved in ethnic disputes or external territorial disputes, including irredentist claims or internal jurisdictional disputes, and if so, they must settle their disputes by peaceful means in accordance with OSCE principles before they get membership.

It might be asked why the Alliance has been so adamant in pursuing such a policy despite its huge cost; meanwhile there is no major power seeking to challenge the Alliance at present and perhaps in the near future; and – over and above this - no significant military benefits can be gained from admitting these small countries. Not only this lack of obvious benefits but also the process itself might, for some, have certain negative repercussions. For instance, Bendow (1998:212) asks: 'What conceivable reason is there for maintaining, and expanding, the quintessential anti-Soviet Alliance, when the Soviet Union no longer exists'. Black (2000:237) considers 'expansion a threatening phenomenon', saying that 'a new world order characterized by a United Nations diminishing in influence and NATO behaving as the world's policeman forces Russian policy planners to re-think their place in the world'.

The answer is to be found in the 1995 'NATO Study on Enlargement', which reached the conclusion that such an enlargement 'is of great importance to the Alliance and is a crucial and fundamental step towards achieving more stable and secure Euro-Atlantic region'. To clarify, the study confirmed that enlargement would lead to:

> Encouraging and supporting democratic reforms, including the establishment of civilian and democratic control over military forces; fostering patterns and habits of co-operation, consultation and consensus-building characteristic of relations among members of the Alliance; and promoting good-neighborly relations.

The study further indicated that:

> The process would increase transparency in defense planning and military budgets, thereby reinforcing confidence among states, and would intensify the overall tendency toward closer integration and co-operation in Europe.

It also concluded that enlargement would increase the Alliance's ability to contribute to European and international security, and strengthen, and broaden the transatlantic partnership. Auton (1998:187) underlines that 'enlargement has been seen as indication of NATO's continued vitality and relevance'.

In assessing this process, it could be argued that it has poured more blood into NATO's vessels. It has sought and led to many positive results, as the 1995 study stated, but first and foremost is the achievement of the Alliance's undeclared target of containing and encircling Russia as much and strongly as possible. What is to be kept in mind in this regard is that Russia remains one of the greatest powers, and still possesses the second largest nuclear arsenal in the world, as well as all the resources which will enable it to play its traditional role in the international arena in the future.

From the American perspective, the enlargement might also serve, in the longer or unforeseen run, as a catalyst for weakening the weight and role of the major European powers, meaning specifically the Germano-French axis, by allowing the 'new' European countries to lobby on the decision making process. Nonetheless, nothing can guarantee that these counties will not change their orientation in the future, once they get absorbed or completely integrated into the strong unified Europe. Brenner (1998:98) suggests that 'in the long run, a progressive Europeanization of NATO is inevitable'.

In any case, the enlargement process, through its criteria and process, has achieved the desired aims, as it has successfully embraced the new members, alleviating suspicion, and erasing the bad memories of historic hostilities. In addition, containing Russia, and giving more 'added value', i.e. more supporting nations, to the Alliance's political and military strength will almost certainly enable it to deter, or even prevent, more efficiently any uncalculated move from another great power, such as gigantic China, in the future.

New confirmation about the success of this process of enlargement was given during the 2006 Riga Summit. Paragraph 29 indicated that:

NATO's ongoing enlargement process has been an historic success in advancing stability, peace and co-operation in Europe and the vision of a Europe whole, free and at peace. In keeping with our pledge to maintain an open door to the admission of additional Alliance members in the future, we reaffirm that NATO remains open to new European members under Article 10 of the North Atlantic Treaty.

Also paragraph 30 states that:

At our next summit in 2008, the Alliance intends to extend further invitations to those countries who meet NATO's performance-based standards and are able to contribute to Euro-Atlantic security and stability.

(IV) -The Partnership For Peace

The second major mechanism introduced by the transformation process was the 'Partnership for Peace' (PFP) programme, which was launched at the 1994 Brussels Summit. Its declared aim was similar to that of the enlargement process, i.e. enhancing stability and security throughout Europe, although it has been different in influence, impact and scope. Since its inception, the programme has been addressed to all states which were members of the North Atlantic Co-operation Council, currently called the Euro-Atlantic Partnership Council, as well as all member states participating in the OSCE, Organization on Security and Co-operation in Europe, that were ready and able to contribute in a positive manner to the programme's activities.

Although membership of this programme can qualify or enable the partners to join the Alliance in future, there is no guarantee that those partners will get membership unconditionally or automatically. In practice, 30 countries have joined the programme since its creation in 1994; ten of which have since become members of the Alliance. In addition, although the programme focuses on defence issues, it gives no security guarantee for partners; however, the Alliance undertakes to consult with any active partner if there is a serious threat against its safety, the security of its territorial integrity and its political independence. In return, the partners must pledge to co-operate in fulfilling the aims and objectives of the programmes which are: to facilitate transparency in national defence planning and budgeting processes; to ensure the democratic control of defence forces; to maintain the capability and readiness to contribute to operations under the authority of the United Nations and / or the responsibility of OSCE; to develop co-operative military relations with NATO for the purpose of joint planning, training and exercises with the aim of strengthening their ability to undertake missions in the field of peacekeeping and humanitarian operations, and to develop, over the longer term, forces that are able to work with the Alliance's forces.

The scope for co-operation is wide and covers a huge spectrum of possibilities, and this enables each partner to choose the activities that suit its needs and abilities. These activities include air defence related matters; airspace management and control; consultation, command and control, interoperability aspects, procedures and terminology; civil emergency planning; crisis management; democratic control of forces and defence structures; defence planning, budgeting and resources management; planning, organization and management of national defence procurement programmes and international co-operation in the armament field; defence policy and strategy; planning, organization and management of national defence research and technology; military geography; global humanitarian mine action; language training; consumer logistics; medical services; meteorological support for NATO-partner forces; military infrastructure; NBCV defence and protection; conceptual planning and operational aspects of peacekeeping; small arms and light weapons; operational, material and administrative aspects of standardization; military exercise and related training activities; military education, training and doctrine. Additionally, NATO has introduced a co-operative science programme that supports collaboration in civil science between scientists from the allies and partnership countries.

To summarize, the main idea lying behind this programme is to engage all the European countries in constant dialogue and co-operation that could, on the one hand, enrich the trust and confidence and, on the other hand, diminish any threat or hostile attitude.

Within the same framework and to meet the required end, the Alliance created another institutionalized forum which is the Euro–Atlantic Partnership Council (EAPC) in order to facilitate regular consultations on political and security issues between NATO members and their partners (all together 46 countries), and allow them collectively and individually to consider the possibilities of co-operation.

Perceivably, the main objective of this mechanism is to convince or seduce governments to re-formalize their policies to be in conformity with the most successful growing military organization worldwide, by taking into consideration that objection or refusal for such co-operation with the Alliance's policies or proposals will not lead to anything but marginalization.

(V) - NATO – Russia /Ukraine partnerships

Arguably, it is imperative not to exclude the defeated or isolated major countries in order to maintain and ensure the durability of any security system. Sperling (1999:186) explains that 'the core requirements of any security order are the possession of legitimacy and the successful assimilation of the defeated states'. Convinced of this, and inspired by the historic experience gained from integrating Napoleonic defeated France into the 'Concert of Europe' more than two hundred years ago, the Alliance took all the necessary precautions, not to provoke or isolate Russia.

It seems that the Alliance has a two-pronged approach to dealing with Russia. The first is containing Russia through the enlargement process, as explained earlier; whereas the second is re-emphasizing the desire and will to get rid of the Cold War way of thinking and replace it with an assurance of sincere desire to co-operate as much as possible in the field of mutual interest. These two factors have left no other alternative for Russia but to co-operate at least for the time being.

Briefly, Russia joined early, in 1991, the North Atlantic Co-operation Council and then the Partnership for Peace (PFP), in 1994, which turned afterwards into the 'Broad, Enhanced Dialogue and Co-operation' relationship. This newly- introduced pattern of co-operation exceeded the limits of the ordinary 'Partnership for Peace'. Co-operation and exchange of information occurred at different levels: ministe-rial, ambassadorial and experts. The most explicit embodiment of this new relationship was the co-operation between the two parties with respect to the implementation of the military aspects of the 1995 peace agreement on Bosnia and Herzegovina. The participation of Russian troops alongside NATO contingents symbolized, at that time, the nature of the new era and its fruitful results and reflected the sincere desire of the two parties to stop being hostages of the old memories of the Cold War.

In a more significant step, the two parties agreed upon what was described as a groundbreaking document, by signing the Founding Act on Mutual Relations, Co-operation and Security between NATO and the Russian Federation, in Paris in 1997. This Founding Act, signed by the heads of state and government, reflected and assured the enduring commitment to jointly working towards building a lasting and inclusive peace in their geographic area, the Euro-Atlantic region, and paved the way to building a peaceful and undivided Europe. Consequently, the NATO-Russia permanent Joint Council (PJC) started its work in 1997, at different levels: ambassadorial and military representatives, plus twice a year at the level of ministers of foreign affairs and defence, and the level of chief of staff. Mutual contact could also be made, as agreed, at the level of heads of state and government. This Council was designated to deal with and address various fields, including political consultations on issues of mutual interest such as the former Yugoslavia; meetings of military representatives; measures to promote co-operation, transparency and confidence, the contribution by NATO and Russia and the role of the PJC in the security architecture of the Euro-Atlantic region; political and defence efforts against the proliferation of weapons of mass destruction; nuclear weapons issues; strategies and doctrines of NATO and Russia; peacekeeping; disarmament and arms control; search and rescue at sea; retraining of military officers; combating international terrorism; defence-related scientific co-operation; defence-related environmental issues; civil emergency planning and disaster relief. Certainly, all these efforts have been exerted to deepen and widen the areas of co-operation between the two ex-adversaries and increase the exchange of expertise in such a way that enriches the culture of rapprochement, and excludes, or at least weakens, the thought of the imperative clash of interests.

As evidence of goodwill and an element of appeasement to some hidden Russian fears and suspicions, Section IV of the Founding Act reiterated the political commitment and undertaking by NATO that 'the allies have not intention, plan, reason, currently and future, to deploy nuclear weapons in the territory of new members of the Alliance'. In fact, it was some sort of reciprocal commitment: the first gave assurance of its peaceful intention and desire not to exclude the latter; while the second undertook to co-operate in certain fields and not to try to block the implementation of the envisaged plan of the Alliance.

However, will it be possible for Russia to obtain full membership of the Alliance in the future? In fact, a world of incessant changes makes predictability too difficult. Nothing can either rule out or support this hypothesis or likelihood for the time being; however, it is still too premature to try to give a definite answer. In this context, David (1999:222) argues that:

> If NATO wants to continue as an organization dedicated to the expansion of a broad community of values and identity – founded on democracy, consensus, and consultation – in Europe, then the inclusion of Russia within the next few decades would appear to be reasonable possibility.

Hyland (1997:161) has previously raised the argument that:

> It would also be wise to use this period to transform the Alliance into a new mechanism for creating a concert of Europe, including Russia, rather than trying to act as the region's policeman or its hegemony.

As long as Russia has not projected its anger or readiness to oppose any of NATO's policies, either close to its borders or worldwide, it can be concluded that the Alliance's policy towards Russia has been successful. This could provide a model which can be applied to other areas, specifically the Middle East region.

As for Ukraine, the NATO-Ukraine Commission was established in order to facilitate regular consultation on security matters, such as the non-proliferation of weapons of mass destruction and civil emergency planning. This was a sort of reward for a 'nuclear country' that accepted voluntarily to get rid of its nuclear capabilities. Given its strategic importance, the Alliance's policy towards Ukraine could be considered as part of the encircling or containing of Russia. Barony (2003:235) quotes former NATO Secretary General Roberston as saying that 'it would probably take another five years before Ukraine could join the Alliance'. Currently, Ukraine is undertaking serious preparations for membership.

(VI) - The NATO- South Mediterranean relationship

Obviously, the Alliance's engagement in Middle Eastern affairs has been one aspect of its huge transformation process. The first ever practical step in this respect was the launching of NATO's dialogue with some of the countries on the southern flank of the Mediterranean, namely Egypt, Israel, Mauritania, Morocco, Tunisia and Jordan in 1995, and Algeria in 2000.

Giving attention to the Mediterranean dimension certainly stemmed from a recognition of the fact that there are huge security challenges, areas of concern and areas of interest that should be cautiously handled through building co-operative relationships with some key moderate states in the region. Lord Robertson (2006:interview) states that:

> There was a mutual interest between the North Atlantic Alliance and the South Mediterranean countries behind launching this process; the Alliance believed that this process could supplement and support the Barcelona process which was seeking to enhance the co-operation in the broader context between the

two parties. Also, the Alliance thought that this process would enable it to "produce influence" in such a manner which could serve its interests.

To elaborate further, Lord Robertson (London 2002) identifies, six main reasons that make the Mediterranean matter to NATO's stability and security:

> The first reason is, of course, its potential of instability, bearing in mind that many crises that affected NATO have in one way or the other originated in and around the Mediterranean; the second reason is terrorism, especially with taking into account that the region, because of its many unresolved political, social, and religious questions, is particularly prone to this menace; the third reason because it is the region that encompasses the Middle East; and without a breakthrough in the Middle East Peace Process, a major obstacle to normalizing Western relations with the Arab world will remain; the fourth reason is that several countries in the Mediterranean region are widely believed to be acquiring weapons of mass destruction; the fifth reason is energy security; as 65 per cent of Europe's oil and natural gas imports pass through the Mediterranean sea which some 3000 ships cross every day, etc; the sixth reason is the economic disparities and their close connection to migration, underlining that since 1986 the per capita income in the Middle East and North African countries has fallen by 2% annually; whereas the population growth rate in the region is 2.5% per year.

He concluded by underscoring the fact that, irrespective of the various definitions of this diverse and complicated region, the Northern and Southern shores of the Mediterranean can not be artificially separated. Furthermore, the deputy SC Rizzo (Rome 2001) points out that 'Many experts predict that the struggle for water could become one of the main sources for conflict in the 21st century; and the Mediterranean region is very much affected by this challenge'.

There has been acknowledgement from both NATO and South Mediterranean countries that, in the post-Cold War era, the growing prominence of Mediterranean security was, and still is, dictating that they should co-operate in good faith for the sake of their individual and mutual interests. These mutual interests include guaranteeing the free and secure flow of oil, taking into account that a large proportion of the crude oil comes from the wider region that includes the Middle East and the Gulf States, and is regularly transported across the Mediterranean, which also contains the major pipeline that links North Africa with Southern Europe. Over and above this, there are countless and inseparable political and economic ties amongst the countries on both sides of the Mediterranean. It seems that the two parties have also recognized that there are certain areas of common interest, whilst recognizing at the same time that there are other areas in which their interests and values might be significantly different.

The NATO-South Mediterranean dialogue was first initiated in 1994 with the aim of contributing positively towards achieving certain general objectives, such as enhancing regional security and stability, improving mutual understanding and dispelling any misconceptions between the Alliance and the Mediterranean dialogue partners. Although it began with a very fluid agenda and rather ambiguous or undefined objectives, the initiative has steadily widened its scope.

The first years of this 'low key' dialogue, were characterized by brainstorming about their prospective relationship and/or a socializing process amongst the officials of the two parties, on different levels, to attempt to enhance mutual understanding. The scope was subsequently extended to develop more opportunities for certain co-operative activities in the areas of military, civil emergency and scientific co-operation. This came about as a direct result of the successive NATO summits giving endorsement to developing or upgrading the relationship between the Alliance and the MD countries.

Certain episodes should be highlighted in the evolution of this dialogue. Two years after its inception, the leaders of the allied countries decided, at the 1997 Madrid Summit, to establish the Mediterranean Co-operation Group to operate under the authority of the North Atlantic Council. Then, the 1999 Washington Summit acknowledged the increasing importance of Mediterranean security, indicating that 'the security of the Alliance as a whole, specifically Europe, is closely linked to the security and stability in this region'. Consequently, it moved towards enhancing the political and practical dimensions of the existing dialogue. More efforts were then exerted to strengthen practical co-operation, particularly with regard to the military dimension, as well as to sharpen political consultations.

To underpin this growing trend, the North Atlantic Council identified, in 2002, strengthening and deepening the relations with the dialogue partners as one of the highest priorities for the Alliance, and then approved certain measures to enhance consultations between the two parties with regard to the issue of terrorism.

At the Prague Summit in 2002, the allies declared in Para 10 that:

> We encourage intensified practical co-operation and effective interaction on security matters of common concern, including terrorism-related issues, as appropriate, where NATO can provide added value......We reiterate that the Mediterranean dialogue

and other international efforts, including the EU Barcelona process, are complementary and mutually reinforcing.

Doubtless, the vital need to trace and uproot terrorism was the reason for 'upgrading and intensifying practical co-operation, etc'. The reference made to the inter-relations and connections between NATO dialogue and the Barcelona process, etc, carried a hidden message that the co-operative dialogue was somehow a pre-condition for gaining the benefits of other regional initiatives.

Therefore, it could be argued that in the aftermath of the events of 9-11, attempts to activate and perhaps maximize the Mediterranean dialogue's potential role gathered momentum. This was especially the case with respect to combating the danger of international terrorism, taking into account the fact that the seven South Mediterranean partners constitute almost half of the Middle East, i.e. half of the existing problem, as perceived by the United States and most of its European allies. Robertson (2006: interview) notes that:

> In the aftermath of 9-11, the Alliance intensified its efforts in combating terrorism; that is why, it was necessary to develop this dialogue to include some practical co-operation, like military exercises with some dialogue partners. Factually, this was done under huge pressure from Italy and Spain because there were more concerned than others because they are nearer to the sources of danger - the Middle East- than other allies.

Also, Alberto Bin (2006: interview) clarifies that:

> This process got a momentum in the years of the twenty-first century; the process has become more active and vital; interest-

ingly, the dialogue partners have started to ask and require, not vice versa, as was the case before.

It is worth mentioning that the North Atlantic Alliance frequently states that the guiding principles governing this MD are: joint ownership between the two parties; non discrimination as well as self-differentiation, which means that although the same levels of discussion and activities were given to all countries, the level of participation may vary from one country to another; complementarities with other international initiatives; and finally progressiveness, which implies that there is always a room for regular enhancement of the dialogue. These overriding principles have granted the dialogue enough flexibility to develop itself, and respond positively, to a certain extent, to the international changes that have occurred in recent years. However, the horizons of the dialogue have been too limited to allow it to serve efficiently the Alliance's full endeavour in this regard. Therefore, new proposals have been recently launched, as will be indicated in the following pages.

CHAPTER THREE

THE DEVELOPMENTS OF POST 9-11 NATO

As a response to the nature of the post 9-11 world, efforts to rejuvenate NATO have acquired new urgency. In short, the Alliance has got the opportunity to prove its validity and ability to perform an indispensable role in securing the Euro-Atlantic region.

In the post 9-11 summits, in Prague, Istanbul and Riga, the allies showed a great determination to set in motion the transformation process to ensure and maximize the Alliance's ability to deal with the repercussions and ramifications of different threats in a changed world, including, first and foremost the scourge of terrorism. Before reviewing the results of the three summits, it is worth clarifying that these seemed to prove that the allies were determined to continue to move together and jump over the fierce differences that erupted between them because of the Iraqi crisis.

I - The Prague summit

Although reference was frequently made to terrorism in most of the documents published from the beginning of the transformation process, it has been listed among the top priorities since the Prague summit of 21 and 22 November 2002, the first ordinary summit convened after the dramatic tragedy of the 9-11 attacks. It seemed as if the Alliance was desperately looking for a justification for its continuation. Previously, Cornish (1997:115) expressed the conviction that:

> Without the coherence and shared purpose imposed by an external threat, all that remains as the basis for the transatlantic security partnership is a general vote of confidence of this sort; NATO has become an "Alliance of choice", rather than an "Alliance of necessity".

To illustrate, the heads of state and government reconfirmed at this summit their determination to combat terrorism, stating in paragraph (4 D, E, F,) of the declaration that: 'terrorism poses a grave and growing threat to Alliance populations, forces and territory as well as to international security; we are determined to combat this scourge for as long as necessary'. They stressed that their response must be multi-faceted and comprehensive including:

> Commitment, in co-operation with partners, to fully implement the Civil Emergency Planning (CEP) Action Plan for the improvement of civil preparedness against possible attacks against the civilian population with chemical, biological or radiological (CBR) agents; enhancing ability to provide support, when requested, to help national authorities to deal with the consequences of terrorist attacks with CBRN against critical infrastructure, as foreseen in the CEP Action Plan; endorsing the implementation of five nuclear, biological and chemical weapons defense initiatives and improving expeditiously the NBC defense capabilities; strengthening the available capabilities to defend against cyber attacks.

These selected activities should not lead to the conclusion that the Alliance is to concentrate only on defensive or precautionary measures. In fact, the Alliance has developed, for the first time, what could be described as a radical change in the structure of its forces. In response to an American request, Paragraph (4-a) indicated that:

> NATO allies have decided to create a NATO Response Force (NRF) consisting of a technological advanced, flexible, deployable, interoperable and sustainable force including land, sea and air elements ready to move quickly to wherever needed, as decided by the council.

It was stated that this force has two aims:

> First, it will provide a high-readiness force able to move quickly to wherever it may be required to carry out the full range of Alliance missions; second, it will be the catalyst for focusing and promoting improvements in the Alliance's military capabilities and, more generally, for their continuing transformation to meet evolving security challenges.

In commenting on this respect, Cehulic (2004:71) explains that:

> U.S policy, on one hand, reduces ESDI significance and operational capabilities within NATO and, on the other hand, creates new NATO forces needed in international actions around the world.

On October 2004, NRF reached its initial operational capability of approximately 17, 000 troops. Recently, in October 2006, it reached its full operational capability with about 21, 000 troops.

Another observation could be made that the use of this force which, practically speaking, cannot be separated from the Alliance's preparedness to deal with terrorism or any states sponsoring or harbouring terrorist groups, will not be linked to or abide by considerations of international legitimacy. Rather it will be 'as decided by the council'. Added to this, the movement of the force will not be limited to the Euro-Atlantic area, but outside it as well, which is a major development in this regard.

At the Riga Summit, it was declared, in paragraph 23 that:

> It also serves as a catalyst for transformation and interoperability and will enhance the overall quality of our armed forces, not only for NATO, but also for EU, UN or national purposes.

This was an attempt to internationalize the purpose, aims, and tasks of this force.

Furthermore, the allies approved a two–fold long-term approach to achieving the required transformation of their troops. In paragraph (4-B), the allies approved an outline plan for a leaner, more efficient, effective and deployable command structure, based on the agreed Minimum Military requirements documents for the Alliance's command arrangement; and in paragraph (4-c) they approved the Prague Capabilities Commitments (PCC):

> As part of the continuing Alliance effort to improve and develop new military capabilities for modern warfare in a high threat environment with highlighting the need for the implementation as quickly as possible

According to the Prague Capabilities Commitments, the individual allies made strong commitments to improve their capabilities in more than 400 specific areas, including, for example, defence against mass destruction and radiological weapons, intelligence and surveillance. The assigned tasks would include:

> Defending common values; respect for democracy and human rights; combating international terrorism and the threat posed by the proliferation of weapons of mass destruction; building security bridges with Russia and Ukraine; further developing the basis for close co-operation with other countries …..and, when other avenues have been exhausted, acting as an effective instrument for managing crises and ensuring that the effects of conflict do not spill over borders or threaten wider stability.

What is more, the allies decided, in paragraph 7, to upgrade co-operation with the Euro-Atlantic Partnership Council (EAPC) and the Partnership for Peace (PFP), and introduce new practical mechanisms, such as 'Individual Partnership Action Plans', which:

> Ensure a comprehensive, tailored and differentiated approach to the partnership, and encourage partners, including the countries of the strategically important region of Caucasus and central Asia to take advantage of these mechanism'.

In addition, they also invited seven countries to become members of the Alliance. Then, in paragraph 10, they outlined their decision to upgrade substantially the political and practical dimensions of the Mediterranean dialogue. Finally, in response to the growing threat from the Middle East region, it was mentioned in paragraph (4-G) that the allies agreed the following:

To examine options for addressing the increasing missile threat to Alliance territory, forces and population centers in an effective and efficient way through an appropriate mix of political and defense efforts, along with deterrence.

II -The Istanbul summit

The Istanbul summit, held on 28 and 29 June 2004, was the first summit convened after the 2003 Iraqi war. It crystallized the enduring commitment of the allies to maintaining the Alliance and a strong determination to face and deter the standing threats with the most appropriate and concerted policies. This summit was a watershed in the evolution of the Alliance, because of its broad-based approach to the issues relating to NATO's policies and transformation mechanisms.

Terrorism was given increasing emphasis at this summit. The European allies needed to show more determination and commitment to combating terrorism, particularly after the explosions in Madrid and Istanbul in the preceding months. At this time, there was no reason not to show as much understanding and tolerance as possible of the robust American policy in this regard. Therefore, it could be argued that the terrorists attacks of Madrid and Istanbul, in a similar way to the 9-11 attacks, rendered the Alliance more coherent and helped to repair, to a great extent, the rift which had occurred as a result of the causes and consequences of the 2003 Iraqi war, and the nature of the American war on terrorism.

Broadly speaking, in Istanbul, the allies agreed to expand their area of interest, as well as the scope of operations, boost the transformation of the Alliance's capabilities and upgrade the existing relationships with the relevant countries on their peripheries. The most important messages and consequences of this summit could be summarized as follows:

1-Terrorism and the proliferation of weapons of mass destruction and their means of delivery, were identified as posing key threats and challenges to the interests of the Alliance, as well as to international security (paragraph 12). This was the clearest indication to date that the Alliance had re-identified its main tasks in such a manner as to ensure its effectiveness in facing either threat or a deadly combination of the two. Paragraph 13 also showed this, stating that 'the Alliance provides an essential transatlantic dimension to the response against terrorism'. The European influence, in this context, was reflected in the affirmation that 'we are committed to continue our struggle against terrorism in all its forms, in accordance with international law provisions and UN principles'. Reference was also made to United Nations' resolution 1373 in the fight against terrorism. This traditional European keenness to stick to international law did not prevent American pressure from imposing another ambiguous formulation. It was stated in the same paragraph that:

> Defense against terrorism may include activities by NATO's military forces, based on decisions by the North Atlantic Council, to deter, disrupt, defend and protect against terrorist attacks, or threat of attacks, directed from abroad, against populations, territory, infrastructure and forces of any member state, including by acting against these terrorists and those who harbor them.

This formula almost overlapped with or abrogated the preceding reference to international law and UN principles by stating that the 'defense decisions will be taken by the North Atlantic Council', not by the authorization of the Security Council. What should be borne in mind here is that 'defense' sometimes requires, according to the new American strategy for national security, 'anticipation' and launching pre-emptive strikes to abort what are perceived to be sources of threats.

Dombrowski & Rayne (2006:115-26) recognize that there is some sort of emerging consensus for preventative war. They also indicate that:

> NATO military authorities have developed a concept that envisions four uses for military force: defensive anti-terrorism to reduce vulnerabilities, consequences management; offensive counter-terrorism and military co-operation; and most notably, counter-terrorism means that NATO is prepared for offensive military action designed to reduce terrorists' capabilities.

2-At the Istanbul summit, the Alliance also added new dimensions to its strategy on combating terrorism, using different diplomatic, political and military means. The declared measures included: improved intelligence sharing between nations; enhanced abilities to respond rapidly to national requests for assistance in protecting against and dealing with the consequences of different sorts of terrorist attacks; providing assistance in protecting selected major events; enhancing contribution to the fight against terrorism by Operation Active Endeavour; exerting robust effort in the Balkans and Afghanistan to help create conditions in which terrorism cannot flourish; enhancing capabilities to defend against terrorist attacks; increasing co-operation with partners, through the implementation of the Civil Emergency Action Plan, the Partnership Action Plan on Terrorism, and contact with other international and regional organizations, such as the active pursuit of consultations and exchange of information with the European Union.

3-Coupled with this, there was more emphasis on the issue of weapons of mass destruction, which were not to be tolerated. The final document set out in detail certain measures that would be taken in this regard, including:

> Supporting NPT and ensuring the full compliance with it by all states party to the treaty; underling the importance of related other international accords; supporting the UNSC 1540 which called on all states to establish national export control etc; strengthening reduction and safeguard nuclear and radiological materials; preventing and containing proliferation of WMD and their means of delivery.

4-Another symptom of the correlation and connectedness between the danger of terrorism and the region of Middle East could be found in paragraph 10. It stated that 'NATO's maritime surveillance and escort operation, Operation Active Endeavour, demonstrates the Alliance's resolve and ability to respond to terrorism', with an indication that the year 2004 had witnessed the extending of the operation to the whole the Mediterranean. What is worth highlighting here is that this operation, to all intents and purposes, violates the sovereignty of some coastal states, although it is going on with the co-operation of some of them. Over and above this, there is no international authorization for such monitoring or intervention.

5- As far as the Middle East region itself is concerned, the document emphasized that it had become an opportune time to address the problem of certain conventional weapons, especially missiles able to reach Alliance territory (paragraph 19). Added to this, it was also declared that a new stage of the relationship between the Alliance and the Middle East in general had begun. More importantly and fundamentally, the allies had decided to enhance the Mediterranean Dialogue and to propose co-operation to the broader Middle East region.

6- The Istanbul summit appeared to affirm that a complex strategic environment requires the continuity of the Alliance, which symbolizes and embodies the transatlantic link between North America and Europe. The view was that the Alliance should continue to serve as both an indispensable forum for consultation between the member states and an effective instrument to defend peace and security. The document implied, consequently, that there should be no reason for, or logic in, expecting any future rift or differences between the European countries and the United States that could threaten the continuity of the Alliance. With respect to the relationship between the Alliance and the European Union, paragraph 26 stated that 'we are pleased with the progress made in developing the NATO-EU strategic partnership on the basis of and since the conclusion of the Berlin + arrangement'. The allies also gave assurances that the two entities were co-operating on a wide range of topics, including security matters, and would continue to do so.

7-The view also prevailed that the Alliance was pursuing, and would continue to pursue, its global and holistic approach in dealing with security issues through different mechanisms, including first and foremost the Partnership, which had a wide geographical scope, extending from Caucasus and Central Asia to the Greater Middle East. In its global role, NATO was, still is, seeking to antagonize nobody; on the contrary, the Alliance would welcome more co-operative and productive relationships with Russia and others. As a demonstration of good faith, the allies agreed to allow 'partners' to increase their contribution to NATO-led operations and participate, to some extent, in the decision making process. The Alliance would also provide them with additional help to reform their militaries, in accordance with NATO's criteria. The newly established Partnership Action Plan on Defense Institution Building, aimed to assist partners to build democratic defence institutions. Again, the implications of the document seemed to be that 'co-operation' was the preferred, if not the 'only available', basis on which others could deal with the Alliance, bearing in mind the Alliance's non-hostile stance. The message was re-inforced that the allies were making the utmost effort to ensure that their Alliance was the most influential and important security organization in the world. In doing this, the Alliance seemed to be providing itself with more 'magnetic power' to attract its partners and pushing them to increase their efforts to develop their policies in such a way that they served the interests of the Alliance.

8-Another observation relating to the Istanbul summit is that the transformation process appeared to be progressing positively, with the Alliance attempting to adapt as fast as it could. For example, NATO's door has remained open to new members, especially Albania, Croatia and the Former Yugoslav Republic of Macedonia. Added to this, the Alliance has been implementing a huge change in its military capabilities and forces, including the streamlining of the command structure so that this can work wherever and whenever the Alliance decides. It is noticeable that emphasis was given to the words 'wherever' and 'whenever', to underline the new extent of the global role of the Alliance.

(III) - The 2005 EU-US Brussels summit

The Brussels Summit was held on 23 February 2005 with the aim of ensuring the indivisibility of the security of the United States and Europe, and underlining the need to work together. Simply, it was another clear message to those concerned that NATO would continue to crystallize the transatlantic Alliance; and the passing frictions would be resolved in time. The EU-US summit was convened in the hope of improving the relations between the two parties and the image of the United States, which had deteriorated significantly as a repercussion of the Iraqi war. At this summit, the US President expressed his confidence in the solidity and strength of the traditional Alliance between Europe and America, based on various uncontestable and unquestionable determinates such as, security considerations, economic co-operation and political and cultural closeness. In his words:

> In a new century, the alliance of Europe and North America is the main pillar of our security; our robust trade is one of the engines of the world's economy; our example of economic and political freedom gives hope to millions who are weary of poverty and oppression.

He concluded by confirming 'no temporary debate, no passing disagreement of governments, no power on earth will ever divide us'. This diplomatic attack was an attempt to refute the arguments of the Europeanists who had been trying to take advantage of the last war to dig a wedge in the long established alliance between Europe and the United States.

In a reciprocal move, the Franco-Germany axis was also keen to show its full adherence to the durability and sustainability of NATO. In his speech, the French president, Jacques Chirac outlined that:

> In the face of today's new challenges, the world needs a strong Alliance, in which Americans and Europeans can combine their efforts in the service of peace; Prague and Istanbul signaled our determination to remodel the transatlantic Alliance on new foundations; adapting our organization to the new realities of the world; in a world fraught with new challenges, out commitment in the service of peace and of our ideals is what makes our alliance fully legitimate; the way to ensure the durability of the strategic partnership forged by the Treaty of Washington

is through a close, steadfast and balanced relationship between America and Europe.

Similarly, former Chancellor Schrader assured that Germany's membership of the Alliance would remain a fundamental element of the national policy and stated that 'NATO continues to be key forum for the discussion of international security issues.' He then called for the continuation of the transformation process of the Alliance and more intensive co-operation with the European Union. Some papers, however, described him as saying that the NATO should no longer be given priority within the framework of the transatlantic Alliance, in general; instead 'it should take the back seat when other issues are to be discussed'.

The two great European countries which fiercely opposed the entanglement of the Alliance in the illegal war in Iraq, were clear in assuring their commitment to the continuation of the Alliance. At the same time, they seemed to imply that the Alliance must adapt to the new realities of the world, which required amongst other things, a balanced relationship between Europe and America. This could indicate that the 'old European countries' were starting to express their unease or a less favourable attitude toward the hegemony of the United States within the Alliance itself.

(IV) - The Riga Summit

The most recent summit, held in Riga, Latvia, 28-29 November 2006, re-confirmed the messages of the previous summits about the indivisibility of security of the 26 member states and their determination to pursue their plans together. It gave special importance to increasing and developing the scope of the existing forms of relationship with non-member states with a view to enhancing the global role of the Alliance. In Paragraph 11, the declaration stated that:

> NATO's policy of partnerships, dialogue, and co-operation is essential to the Alliance's purpose and its tasks. It has fostered strong relationships with countries of the Euro-Atlantic Partnership Council (EAPC), the Mediterranean Dialogue (MD), and the Istanbul Co-operation Initiative (ICI), as well as with Contact Countries. NATO's partnerships have an enduring value, contributing to stability and security across the Euro-Atlantic area and beyond. NATO's missions and operations have also demonstrated the political and operational value of these relationships: eighteen nations outside the Alliance contribute forces and provide support to our operations and missions, and others have expressed interest in working more closely with NATO.

The heads of states and government requested the Council in Permanent Session to further develop this policy, in particular to:

A) fully develop the political and practical potential of NATO's existing co-operation programmes: EAPC/Partnership for Peace (PfP), MD and ICI, and its relations with Contact Countries, in accordance with the decisions of our Istanbul Summit;

B) increase the operational relevance of relations with non-NATO countries, including interested Contact Countries; and in particular to strengthen NATO's ability to work with those current and potential contributors to NATO operations and mission, who share our interests and values.

C) increase NATO's ability to provide practical advice on, and assistance in, the defence and security-related aspects of reform in countries and regions where NATO is engaged.

Moreover, the 2006 Riga summit called for the continuation of defence transformation in order to increase the efficiency of the Alliance in deterring the 21st century contingencies. In this respect, they endorsed a set of initiatives (paragraphs 22, 23, 24).

Again, reference was made to the point that 'our operations in Afghanistan and the Balkans confirm that NATO needs modern, highly capable forces that can move quickly to wherever they are needed upon decision by the NAC'. Noticeably, no mention of the role of Security Council was made in this respect. It seems clearer than ever that 'decision by the NAC' is the most important if not the only factor in determining the Alliance's moves on the world stage.

Having reviewed the different aspects, mechanisms and stages of the transformation process, one can conclude that the transformation of the North Atlantic Alliance following the end of the Cold War has been remarkable. During the 1990s, starting from the July 1990 London Summit, which heralded a Europe 'whole and free', and culminating in the decisions of the Washington Summit in April 1999, the Alliance made major changes to its composition as well as a tremendous shifts in its policies. Another stage of the accelerated transformation process can be seen as beginning after the events of 9-11. The whole process has attempted to ensure that the Alliance remains indispensable for the safety and security of the Euro-Atlantic region. In short, the result has been the maximization of NATO's strength, enlargement of its scope and globalization of its new role. Yet, there are several arenas which need to be kept in harmony and a number of issues to be resolved to ensure the continuing success of the Alliance. The major impacts of the transformation process include the following:

A - NATO has become an organization that can deal with a broad range of security issues that exist far beyond its own geographical area. The limited defence nature of its role was replaced by an anticipative, even offensive, role by which the Alliance can move to deter, not only within the territories of the Euro-Atlantic Alliance, but also worldwide upon the decisions of the allies; meaning wherever and wherever they deem it necessary. This self-given mandate means only one thing: that today's NATO is completely different from the one that existed before.

B - The Alliance has assumed a diplomatic role or duties after transforming itself from a military body concerned with defence-related issues to a military-political and security organization that has a comprehensive competence and jurisdiction.

C- The importance given to international law and the role of the United Nations has been decreased significantly since the Kosovo operation. The Alliance has come to recognize that it cannot, sometimes, afford to wait for prolonged political consultation and agreement. Although it has certain logic which could be justifiable or understandable, it is appears that this trend fails to give due respect to international legitimacy. This trend has been reinforced by the policies of the 'The United States" since the 9-11 events.

D- The holistic approach of the transformation process was flexible enough to increase tremendously the importance and weight given to the Middle East region, especially in the aftermath of the attacks of 9-11. Without doubt, the region has become the top priority of the Alliance.

CHAPTER FOUR

NATO's Resilience

I - Passing the crossroad

Despite all these cataclysmic changes, some still cast doubt on the continuity of the Alliance arguing that it is at a crossroads and going through a transitional period that might carry the seeds of its own dissolution. Plainly, there are some flaws in the current transatlantic relationship, giving some grounds to question the durability of the Alliance in the coming decades. This seems to be a direct result of the nature of the post 9-11 U.S policies.

Evidently, the post 9-11 'United States 'has been unwilling to be constrained within the framework of multilateral Alliances such as NATO, so it has sought to create its own 'coalitions of the willing' for some specific missions abroad. For some analysts, this policy may underline the 'hidden or ignored' perception that has existed in Alliance circles for several years, but would have been vehemently denied, that NATO's role has gradually, but steadily, diminished since the end of the Cold War. Boot (2004:5) observes that: Even before the current controversy over Iraq, it was already obvious that the NATO Alliance was too large and too unwieldly to take effective military action'. Talbott (2002) says that 'current NATO might be at risk; fresh paint can no longer hide cracks in the plaster along the winding corridors.

Controversially and interestingly, 9-11 itself was a standing dilemma for the North Atlantic Alliance. Lansford (2002:180) notices that 9-11 was a watershed in the Alliance's history saying that:

> To the detractors of the Alliance, American domination of the military campaign in Afghanistan and the relegation of the allies to conducting support missions for the US seemed to demonstrate the fading utility of NATO.

On the other hand, he adds:

> The invocation of Article 5 and the wide range of military and non-military actions taken by the Alliance confirmed the continuing centrality of NATO to the supporters or the organization.

This uncertain situation has created an undefined vacuum which begs a number of questions. These questions include: What will the Alliance look like in the coming decades?; Is NATO able to serve as a full-spectrum Alliance in the twenty first century?; Will the European Defense and Security Identity present itself as, or constitute, an alternative to the Alliance?; Will this EU identity collide with the role of the Alliance?; Will the EU-American rift ruin the Alliance in the future? Obviously, all these unanswered questions are opening up for discussion the adequacy of the North Atlantic Alliance in the twenty first century.

To begin with, some predict the collapse or even failure of the Alliance in assuming its international role because of the growing gap that is separating the two pillars of the transatlantic Alliance. For example, Bronstone (2000:81) expresses doubts about the future of the transatlantic Alliance itself, taking into account the geo-strategic consequences of the enlargement of the Alliance, saying that:

> How much does the assertion of the transatlantic Alliance being a stable relationship in spite of the many episodic crises hold true in the post Cold War world of uncertainty, instability, and one where there is a lack of common enemy?

He concludes that 'at the end of the day, it may be true that 'the West' was never one, and because of that, it will never be one after the process of enlargement.'

Carpenter (2001:22-4) has expressed the conviction that the widening fissures in the transatlantic security relationship cannot be concealed – much less repaired – by language in the new strategic concept, arguing that:

> The continuing disagreement about NATO's mission and the proper division of labor raise a possibility that NATO partisans understandably do not want to confront the fact that perhaps the Alliance is in fact irrelevant to the security environment of post Cold War Europe.

Furthermore, Layne (2001:79) suggests that:

> While there is no common external threat to hold the fissiparous forces at bay and keep the Alliance together, the fact that the

United States and Europe are destined to drift apart strategically and politically is no longer open to doubt.....the only issue is how this distancing occurs.

On the contrary, some maintain that the transatlantic Alliance can prove its necessity and durability currently and in the future. For example, Voigt (2004:180) holds the view that:

Contrary to what the prophets of doom have been predicting, the Atlantic has not grown wider in recent years; quite the opposite: the differences we are seeing now are signs of constantly increasing closeness, of a quasi -domestic relationship across the Atlantic.

This is because of many factors, he further argues, among them that 'not a single problem in the world can be solved if Europe and the United States are at odds'.

Gheciu (2005:238-40) points out that:

In the first decade after the end of the Cold War, NATO defined itself and secured international recognition – as not just a military alliance but also the institutional expression of the Western community of liberal democratic values and norms; following the September 11 terrorist attacks, NATO again invoked its identity as the key security institution of the Western community, in an attempt to ward off challenges to its relevance in the context of the war on terror.

Furthermore, Serfaty (2004:86) draws attention to 'the limits of NATO as the security institution of choice'. He confirmed, however, 'its unparallel potential over that of any ad-hoc Alliance was reinforced by the events of September 11, 2001', meaning that no ad-hoc coalition can replace or undermine the North Atlantic Alliance in practical terms.

Others confirm the vitality of the Alliance and call for further extension of its scope. Daalder (2006) observes that:

> Creating a global NATO is not about saving the Alliance from obsolescence, but to meet the global challenges…. NATO has to be a truly global alliance by extending its membership to any democratic state, like Australia, Brazil, and Japan etc., so that it can play a role in fulfilling its new duties.

These contradictory views reflect, in essence, the complexity of the current debate in this regard. In the following analysis, I will review the causes and features of the current position of NATO, in an attempt to be able to predict the determinates of the future of the North Atlantic Alliance.

To begin with, it could be noted that there has been, in some measure, an unorganized, perhaps weak, opposition, especially in Europe, to the continuity of the Alliance in the post Cold War world, i.e. in the nineties and at the beginning of the twenty first century. The main argument of this opposition has been based on the perception that nothing could justify the tremendous expenditure on the developments and amendments in the structure of the Alliance in the absence of any serious threat. However, this view has been largely overwhelmed by the huge efforts on the part of the United States to put the continuation and transformation of the Alliance among the top priorities of its foreign policy. These efforts gained the support and encouragement of some major European powers for different reasons.

After the 1999 Washington summit, a milestone in the Alliance's history, the idea seemed to be that NATO, which had never been examined or tested before, would be developed in such a manner as to make it the guarantor of the allies' security in the twenty first century. This was agreed upon regardless of the reiteration of certain arguments about the future of a unified Europe and its armed organ, or existing confusion about the limits of the Alliance's role and its governing criteria.

The frequent saying that 'everything changed after September 11' could be valid in the case of NATO as well, but only for couple of years. To expand on this, the emergence of a new global era of countering international terrorism, following the September 11 attacks, has fundamentally changed the primary threats to international security and redefined the concept of security for all states, although in different ways. The Alliance responded swiftly, in a manner that embodied the solidarity of the allies, and, at the same time, its vitality and necessity in this new and un-defined era. This was crystallized in the declaration, made on September 12, for the first time in the Alliance's history, about the readiness of NATO to invoke Article 5, which states that:

> The Parties agree that an armed attack against one or more of them in Europe or North America shall be considered an attack against them all and consequently they agree that, if such an armed attack occurs, each of them, in exercise of the right of individual or collective self-defense recognized by Article 51 of the Charter of the United Nations, will assist the Party or Parties so attacked by taking forthwith, individually and in concert with the other Parties, such action as it deems necessary, including the use of armed force, to restore and maintain the security of the North Atlantic area.

This appeared to be a somehow symbolic move in an atmosphere of high tension that presented irrefutable evidence of mutual and unconditional commitment between allies, and put another wedge in the workings of an opposition camp which appeared to be seeking to end the role of the Alliance. To translate this will into action, the Alliance embarked on a hot pursuit mission in the Mediterranean Sea to monitor and inspect the ships. From that point on, NATO members collectively defined terrorism as a primary threat, and reconfirmed the utility and ability of the Alliance in providing common defence against it to an extent that led some analysts to raise the argument that defeating terrorism could be the new raison d'être for NATO in a post 9-11 world.

However, 'everything changed' again in 2003 and this new momentum has been lost because of the nature of the American policy in its war against terrorism in general and the ramifications of the Iraqi war in particular. In this context, Kaplan (2004: 143) strongly believes that 'the Iraq issue conceivably could have been the rock on which the Atlantic Alliance might split in two, or collapse altogether'.

Once more, the future of the Alliance has become an area of fierce contention and doubt, especially in Europe. Obviously, the conflict-ing views toward the legality and necessity of this war have led to a complete division between the allies that was reflected in the inability of the North Atlantic Council to reach consensus over the US request for support in the event of war. In addition to this, Belgium, France and Germany imposed a veto in March 2003, on the commencement of military planning to defend another member state, Turkey, in the event of hostilities with Iraq. Some European allies, specifically France and Germany, were adamant in refusing any entanglement of the Alliance in this war because of its illegality in terms of international law. The opposition group deemed that, in waging a hostile or pre-emptive war to achieve regime change in Iraq, in full negligence of international legitimacy, the United States went far beyond actions in which a defensive alliance could be of assistance and, in actual fact violated the rules of decision making within NATO.

What is more, it is worth underlining that other aspects of the new robust American interventionist policy worry the Europeans, as well as others worldwide, who have sought to distance themselves from, if not resist, such a policy which incites global hatred and antagonism. To clarify, Haass (2002) explains that:

> The attacks on the World Trade Center and the Pentagon did not create the post-post-Cold War world; but they helped end the decade of complacency; they forced Americans to see clearly that foreign policy still matters, and that our oceans and our ICBMs alone do not make us safe; they brought home the stark reality that if we do not engage with the world, the world will engage with us, and in ways we may not like; so, on September 11, our innocence ended, and we entered the post-post-Cold War world, a period when increasingly potent transnational challenges intersect with still important traditional concerns.

He further adds that:

> It is especially important for the United States to have a cogent foreign policy approach because the United States is -- and will remain into the foreseeable future -- the world's pre-eminent power according to every metric -- military, economic, political, or cultural, confirming that the United States will continue to affect the shape of international relations and their trajectory more than any other country.

Also, Simpson (2004) explains that one fallout of the war against Iraq relates to perceptions about America's increasing heavy-handedness, and recalls that:

> US Secretary of Defense Rumsfeld recently threatened to pull NATO headquarters out of Brussels unless Belgium agreed to repeal a law which gives its courts universal jurisdiction to try cases of genocide, war crimes and human rights violations; while Belgian parliamentarians did agree to change the law (to cases in which either the victim or the accused were residents of Belgium), war crimes lawsuits had already been filed against US President George Bush, UK Prime Minister Tony Blair, US Secretary of State Colin Powell, General Tommy Franks, and Secretary of Defense Donald Rumsfeld.

Perhaps justifiably, some have jumped to the conclusion that the rift created by the Iraqi war, as well as the other policies of the new conservative ruling elite in Washington, could be irredeemable, particularly given that two determinates have been emerging and moving simultaneously although in different directions. The first is the Franco-German axis, which has been persistent about building an independent European security and defence policy, regardless of the hesitation of Britain and other US-friendly new European countries. The second is that Washington has, undeniably, become eager to ignore its alliance and allies in favour of building ad-hoc coalitions through which it can apply its policies without the necessary consensus and consultation that have hitherto characterized the performance of the 55-year-old organization. In their assessment, this could amount to irrefutable proof that the Alliance has become obsolete, even in the eyes of its leader, and could not constitute, currently, more than a toolbox which the United States can use or ignore it whenever it wants. It is noteworthy that what constitutes some sort of weakness and causes a lack of urgency in the

Alliance's performance, at least from the American perspective, is its decision-making mechanism, which is based on consensus and requires that all decisions must be unanimous.

Most importantly, the issue of pre-emption remains a complex and divisive one. The question which should be raised at this point is whether or not European countries can accept the doctrine of pre-emption that is the backbone of the new strategy for U.S national security, to be applied without necessarily having recourse to international legitimacy. Again, to attempt to answer this question now might be premature, especially in the case of the liquidity that has characterized the trans-atlantic relationships since the 2003 Iraqi war. Covina (2003) draws attention to this dilemma saying that:

> Pre-emption is a part of the US National Security Strategy but has been little discussed in NATO; so a thorough going debate on preemption will sooner or later have to take place in NATO and this debate will have to be reflected in our next strategic doctrine.

Despite all these factors, it does seem that, in essence, the United States has succeeded in heading off the repercussions of the Iraqi crisis. There are many possible reasons for this, among them its having sought international legitimacy for its occupation of Iraq, and worked successfully with some European allies to overcome what was seen as a rift in the Transatlantic Alliance. This shows that the differences between the Alliance's two pillars did not reach the point of 'no return'. As demonstrated at the Brussels summit, as well as preceding summits, common interests and mutual benefits have surpassed any existing differences, at least for the time being. Also, there is a noticeable change in the US attitudes towards NATO. Lindley (2006) indicates that:

On Capitol hill and in the Pentagon the Alliance is sometimes regarded as an anachronistic side-show, ill-suited and under-equipped to play any meaningful role in America's grand strategic mission to bring stability and prosperity to the world through democracy.........For a brief political moment, neo-conservatism threatened to replace American's internationalism with unilateralism, as Americans played with the idea that the US was indeed more powerful than the rest of the post 9-11 world; but with the challenges posed by Afghanistan and Iraq, that moment has passed, and it is once again to the mature democracies, most of which are in Europe, that the American people look instinctively for support.

In line with this, the declared position, frequently repeated by high officials of both sides, as well as NATO's Secretary General, was that the allies agreed to overlook their differences over Iraq and resume 'moving together'. As evidence of having overcome its crisis, the Alliance assisted the multinational division led by Poland to be a stabilizing force in south-central Iraq, in co-operation with the American and other coalition forces there. It also provided training for the new Iraqi security forces. In brief, it could be confirmed that NATO has successfully survived the 2003 crisis.

II -NATO and the challenge of the ESDI

Factually, there has been a widening gap in military capabilities between Europe and the United States. It seems interesting that while some believe that this imbalance may decrease the Alliance's efficiency in assuming its role internationally, others are convinced that NATO will face a very serious threat to its existence if the Europeans intend to bridge this 'gap' by redoubling efforts to forge their own common defence and security policy. To make it clearer, there is a view that the growing European Security and Defense Identity will encourage the Europeans to move towards choosing their own manner in addressing the pressing security challenges, away from the major influence of the United States. It can be argued that this may ultimately inflict more weakness on the body of the Alliance. With regard to this, Tonelson (2001:47) observes that:

> The end of the Cold War should have represented a golden opportunity for the European allies to narrow and even close the security gaps between their military forces and their security challenges, but the European continued to respond to the transformed security landscape simply by shrinking their militaries.

Missiroli and Quille (2004:131-4) point out that:

> While the Iraqi crisis highlighted the weakness and fragility of European defense and security policy, and underlined the fact that the EU has no reliable military capabilities at its own disposal, it will prompt the European member States to articulate a particular and coherent European approach, bearing in mind that current significant command and control capabilities shortfalls among them means that any complex, high-end operation would have to depend on NATO support.

As far as the current ESDI is concerned, it is worth noting that this has been for a long time an issue of great concern and sensitivity for all concerned parties, i.e. the Europeans and Americans, although it has been shrouded in the kind of diplomatic language used by the high-ranking officials on both sides. Perhaps, no other issue has been overshadowed by this amount of ambiguity. Carpenter (2001:2-20) notes that:

A major portion of America's political and policy elite was openly unenthusiastic about ESDI, fearing that it would automatically become a competitor to NATO and dilute Washington's influence in the overall transatlantic relationship.

He also adds that 'US inconsistency, if not hypocrisy, on the ESDI issue began to raise European emotions to the boiling points in early 2000'. At this point, it should perhaps be mentioned that, the United States, through ex-Secretary of State Madeline Albright, declared that:

> 3 D's are to be taken by Europeans to ensure that ESDI doesn't undercut NATO which are: this ESDI must not diminish the role of the Alliance, must not duplicate NATO's capabilities, and must not discriminate against the United States.

Presumably, American suspicion of the European intention in this regard has escalated recently. More specifically, Larrabee (2004: 38) highlights that:

> The proposal by France, Germany, Belgium, and Luxembourg at the controversial mini –summit in April 2003 to establish a separate EU operational planning headquarter in Tervuren provoked a strong negative reaction in Washington.

He cited the US permanent representative to NATO calling the plan "one of the most serious dangers to the transatlantic relationship".

In a similar vein, Burns(2003) emphasises that:

> The agreement for the co-operation between the EU and NATO requires that there should not be no new military headquarters

to compete with NATO; and no new planning authority to compete with SHAPE, etc.

Also, Brenner (1998:102-3) warned that 'giving life to ESDI can not fail to generate Euro-American tension'.

Certainly, European keenness to develop an autonomous EDSI did not emerge without reasonable incentives. To illustrate, the Alliance has lost, practically speaking, some of its strategic importance for some major European powers. Although the post 9-11 terrorism presents the Euro-Atlantic nations with a complex, deadly and persistent threat that requires the combined efforts of all the allies to form a multilateral strategic response involving many policy dimensions, some hold the view that mutual security needs are no longer as essential as they were during the Cold War. Hyde-Price (2000-143-165) thinks that 'for contemporary Germany, NATO's utility is more political than military', arguing that:

> Article V security guarantees are no longer as vital for German security as they were during the Cold War; consequently, the relative significance for German security policy of other security institutions such as the EU and OSCE has grown.

That is why one can find Germany, as well as France which is usually at the forefront of moves to realise the new unified Europe, more enthusiastic about the growth of an independent European identity.

These arguments aside, it is noticeable that both parties seem keen to promote the idea that NATO and ESDI can serve one another, and move closer with the passing of time. Subsequently, since its inception, the relation between the EU defence and security policy with that of

NATO has been evolving slowly but steadily. In December 2002, the EU and NATO signed a statement confirming the need for effective mutual consultation and co-operation, and stressing equality and due regard for the decision-making autonomy and interests of the both entities.

The most significant development in this respect was reaching the 'Berlin Plus' formula. On 17 March 2003, the EU and NATO signed the 'Berlin Plus' arrangement, which fosters co-operation between the two entities and sets rules, allowing the EU military mission to resort to NATO capabilities. Harle (2006:71-5) points out that 'Berlin Plus has received high marks due to a number of innovative structural changes within NATO and the EU'. He rules out a clash of interests between the two organizations for a number of reasons, including the existence of political will and the fact that NATO and the EU operate in rather different ways, 'while NATO exclusively deals with security policy, the latter represents only one of many EU policy areas'. Smith (2006:65-6) commends 'Berlin Plus', but indicates that, it has also had its share of challenges. She illustrates this saying that:

> Because two members of the European Union who are not members of NATO (Cyprus and Malta) lack the necessary security clearance, virtually no intelligence sharing takes place between the two organizations, and this issue has not only affected 'Berlin Plus', but it also impacts every aspect of the EU-NATO relationship and paralyzes joint initiatives.

Apart from this, there are a number of factors that, practically speaking, exclude the possibility of a 'big' clash of interests between the two entities. Firstly, 19 countries out of the 25 members of the EU and 26 members of NATO are members of both organizations; therefore, there is only a remote probability of friction between the two organizations at least on strategic matters. Secondly, the 2003 EU Security Strategy identified five threats – terrorism, weapons of mass destruction, failed states, regional conflicts and organized crime. This means that the aims of the EU Security Strategy are almost identical or similar to those of NATO's doctrine. Consequently, an argument could be made that the similarity of objectives could weaken the possibility of policy contradictions. Thirdly, the new NATO allies, 'new Europe', which are captives of US influence, will get the opportunity to strengthen their relations and increase their influence within the EU and NATO. In other words, the 'growing' American influence will tie the two organizations together. Robertson (2006:interview) states:

> I don't accept the assumption that the growing EDSI would threaten the continuity of the Alliance; on the contrary, it will enable the Europeans to assume more responsibilities and shoulder more burden within the framework of the Alliance.

Quinlan (2001: 81) expresses the conviction that:

> The positive advantages of a successful ESDP for EU and its members, present and prospective, need no underlining ; and the Atlantic Alliance too will be strengthened and its balance made healthier, if better European contribution is forthcoming.

The case of Afghanistan, in which European forces replaced Alliance forces upon the completion of its task is presented as a proof of the 'healthy' co-operation between the two entities. It can be predicted that this will inspire both organizations to repeat the same experience in the future. Another example which has frequently been mentioned as one of most fruitful co-operative operations between the two entities is the case of the former Yugoslav republic of Macedonia, in which the forces of both NATO and EU joined together in efforts aimed to prevent the expected civil war.

However, this matter is not quite so straightforward or transparent and cannot be judged on the goodwill of the concerned parties. Cornish (1997:115) explains that:

> The compromise agreed at Berlin in June 1996 and developed thereafter is one which deals with the present without closing off other options, including the future development of a European identity.

Factually, there are some outstanding issues which are far from clear and need to be resolved in order to pave the way towards a stable relationship between them. To start with, the existing arrangements for co-operation between the Alliance and the ESDI within the framework of the 'Berlin Plus' formula may not, ultimately, sit well with the emerging European identity. Other unresolved issues include participation on non-European allies in EU defence matters; and the required arrangements to increase transparency and avoid the duplication of the two entities; and how the nascent NFR and the EU Rapid Reaction Force (RRF) will interact and co-operate in the future. So, there may be symptoms of unease in building up the current relationship between NATO and the EU, hidden, diplomatically, between lines. SG Scheffer (2006) observes that:

> The NATO-EU relationship is currently suffering from under-stretch rather than overstretch; NATO and EU need a sustained dialogue about harmonizing their military transformation, notably the NRF and the EU battle groups. Our organizations also need to get away from replicating each other's 'initiatives; if NATO or the EU has come up with a worthwhile project, the

other institution should not seek to create a similar initiative, but rather support the one that exists; NATO and the EU are in the business of security, not engaged in a beauty contest.

Gardner (2002:79-80) indicates that:

> Although there is no unified European position on EU-NATO security relationship, most EU members want more EU decision-making power, planning capacity, and operational capability for military crisis management in Europe; in this case, NATO and the EU will find themselves in a new type of independent relationship.

Given the nature of the current relationship, one can argue that there is a degree of reluctance to establish an early and transparent EU-NATO working partnership, especially with regard to such areas as defence planning and criteria for conducting joint operations. This reluctance is doubtless a normal result of the moderate, if not modest, European weight in the decision-making process within NATO circles, in comparison with the huge influence of the United States. It most likely also reflects American keenness not to make the Alliance a scapegoat for the good of the 'European super-state' in the future. Bluth & Kirchner (1995:13) maintain that:

> The development of a European defense identity had been hampered by the existence of a variety of competing institutional frameworks, none of which fulfilled all the perceived requirements of European defense or was superior to the existing framework of defense-co-operation.

Significantly, while some deem that a stronger Europe will produce a stronger NATO, in accordance with the view of 'separable but not separate', it is not self-evident that an autonomous ESDI can be reconciled with NATO's primacy, i.e. always conceding priority to the Alliance. The 2002 U.S strategic concept, page 11, clarified that the current American position upholds the vision that NATO should and would be given the utmost priority, and then, and only after that can the Europeans conduct their own operations by their own means, provided that they should have got, first, the appropriate consent and support of NATO. This will certainly always require the approval of the United States; thus, it could be argued that Europe will not, most probably, be able to complete or apply a fully independent and autonomous policy, away or apart from US influence in the foreseeable future.

From another perspective, there are some conflicting views about forging a unified coherent European policy in this regard. Optimists argue that the experience of recent years has shown that European power is not only confined to soft power; therefore, it can produce an efficient EDSI. In fact, the European Security and Defense Policy has made significant progress. To illustrate, the EU countries have made about 60.000 troops available to the European Union according to the 2001 Helsinki Headline Goals. Also, the EU has carried out operations in such locations as Macedonia and the Congo. On this subject, Giegerich & Wallace (2004:163-4) observe that 'there has been a remarkable increase in the scale, distance and diversity of external operations by European forces'. They highlight the fact that:

> The EU governments were standing 50, 000-60, 000 troops on operations outside their common boundaries, in more than 20 countries in southeast Europe, Afghanistan, and Central Asia, Iraq and the Gulf, and Africa, and if the contributions of European non-EU members of NATO are included the numbers

deployed during the past year rise to an average of around 70, 000 and a peak (including the British deployment to Iraq) approaching 90, 000.

In contrast, some take the view that nothing, currently, can confirm that the Europeans will be able achieve the optimal version of their EDSI in the coming years. This is due to various factors, including: a stronger European defence identity cannot be formulated and built without Britain which is the greatest ally of the United States; a change in power has occurred in Germany; the defeat of Europeanists in a referendum about the European constitution in France, etc, and the inability of the democratically elected government to increase military allocation while facing many social and economic problems.

Sangiovanni (2003:202-4) believes that:

> The ESDP has little chance of re-balancing the Atlantic Alliance or of reversing American unilateralism, as the French would like; it will not significantly improve transatlantic burden-sharing, thereby placating the British, nor will it have beneficial side effects such as propelling the EU faster towards a federal union, as the Germans may have hoped for; instead, it risks triggering a US withdrawal from Europe before Europeans have found a viable defense substitute; it risks undermining the EU's capacity for non–military crisis management; and it puts enlargements at risk by exacerbating divisions among current and future member states.

Sangiovanni goes on to suggest that Europeans should instead focus on strengthening their capacity for what they do best, namely non-military crisis management and post-war reconstruction.

In addition, what should not be underestimated is that the admission of new 10 members to the EU has added more complexity. Put quite simply, this has changed the centres of gravity, atmosphere and priorities. Jones (2003) notes that:

> The EU has at last reached a stage where the differences between the member states are too great to bridge; and the resulting conflict between large and small, rich and poor, has shattered consensus on the basic rules for decision-making.

What should be borne in mind here is that EU decision-making in the security and defence sector is by consensus.

Over and above this, the huge financial cost of the project adds more complexity and makes its success uncertain. It can be argued that, at a time of declining military budgets, the only way to address the shortfalls and standing threats is through closer co-operation between the EU and NATO, by developing a higher degree of mutual interdependence or defence integration, not by seeking to create a fully independent identity. Simon and Kery (1999:382-2) raise the argument that:

> The idea of a fully independent ESDI is impractical if not lack of logic, indicating to the results of Rand Corporation Study that the loWest level of independent military capability is estimated at $ 27 billion over twenty-five years and still would require the aid of the US system to make it function; whereas the highest level of independent ESDI activity would cost $95 billion over the twenty five years; and higher level would be more effective, but it still would not equal the capabilities now available in NATO.

Thies (2003:11) points out that 'democracies are reluctant to spend money on defense'. In the same vein, Alberto Bin (2006: interview) opines that:

> From the pragmatic perspective, I don't see the growing ESDI would threaten the continuity of the Alliance; this is because the democratically elected governments will find it too difficult to justify to the public opinion the increase in the military expenditure to create another parallel organization similar to NATO ; Meanwhile, there is no strong incentives for this endeavour; and there are still huge standing social problems like unemployment.

Necas (2004) notes that:

> When we look at our Europe as a whole, it is clear that we need to be able to do two types of military operations: firstly, stability operations such as those in the Baltic, with or without NATO, and secondly, high-end operations with NATO; and it is hard to imagine a scenario requiring true high-military force where NATO would not be involved and when Europe is.

Some believe that the fruitful co-operation between the two entities is an imperative choice for both of them and perhaps the most likely future scenario. Gordon (2005) argues that:

> Although NATO is still vital, it is by itself too narrow to handle the full range of co-operation needed in the years ahead; in the evolving Europe, the EU will become responsible for key areas of transatlantic co-operation – from homeland security to democracy promotion to humanitarian assistance.

Gordon adds:

> NATO remains a key forum and the institution of choice for acting militarily and needs to be more closely connected to the EU to ensure the proper coordination of overall policy and strategy.

Most recently, the need to 'strive' to improve the existing relationship between the two entities was recognized at the latest summit (2006). Paragraph 41 states that:

> NATO and the EU share common values and strategic interests. NATO-EU relations cover a wide range of issues of common interest relating to security, defence and crisis management, including the fight against terrorism, the development of coherent and mutually reinforcing military capabilities and civil emergency planning. Our successful co-operation in the Western Balkans, including through the Berlin Plus arrangements regarding EU operation Althea, is contributing to peace and security. We will strive for improvements in the NATO-EU strategic partnership as agreed by our two organisations, to achieve closer co-operation and greater efficiency, and avoid unnecessary duplication, in a spirit of transparency and respecting the autonomy of the two organisations. A stronger EU will further contribute to our common security.

III - The Future of NATO

Twenty-first century NATO is neither broken nor marginalized, at least for the time being. Supported by the weight of the 'American empire' and most of the European allies, the Alliance is entering a new era. After getting through the repercussions of the Iraqi crisis, it is now addressing old as well as new security threats. NATO now is functioning operationally in three continents and about 50, 000 soldiers are deployed under its command. Its diverse activities are being conducted in a large area, stretching from Kosovo westward to Afghanistan eastward, and from the Mediterranean and Iraq upwards to Darfur downwards.

Robertson (2006:interview) asserts:

> I can confirm that the Alliance will always have the precedence or priority in handling the issues which the allies agree upon them; this is because no other organization in the world, including the United Nations itself, has the capabilities which the Alliance possesses; the proof is in the recent roles of the Alliance in Afghanistan and Darfur.

Extrapolating into the near future, it is very unrealistic to expect the dissolution of the North Atlantic Alliance, at least in the coming two decades, for various strategic and fundamental reasons. The first and foremost is the increasing sense of insecurity worldwide, whether this is the result of realities on the ground or illusions in the mind. The idea of a 'world of insecurity' is continually gaining ground. In a 2003 Gallup International Poll, that was conducted in 51 countries, almost half of those who were questioned expressed the conviction that the next generation would live in a more insecure world and almost twice as many respondents rated global security as poor as those who described it as good.

Certainly, the changes that have occurred in the geo-strategic context have had, and will continue to have, a direct impact on NATO's role and strategy. Haseler (2003:12-20) suggests that the death of the 'current' NATO is a result of the ramifications of the last Iraqi war, arguing that a new independent European security system with its own doctrine will, obviously, mean that the current structure and purpose of NATO will need to be revised from a military and political Alliance into a primarily political Alliance. He deems that the new Alliance would stress the underlying political, social and cultural unity of Europe and America, and retain the clause in which each signatory remains committed to come to the defence of the others in case of attack. Lieven (2003:298) argues that:

> It seems quite possible that as the first decade of the twenty first century progresses, NATO will take a long stride away from its old function as a hard military Alliance for mutual defense, and toward becoming a much 'softer' kind of mainly political grouping.

Coker (2002:71) states that 'NATO could be more accurately described as a risk community that secures the interests of its members against the new global insecurity they face'. Furthermore, Rynning (2005:169-79) ascribes NATO's continuity to the political commitment to transatlantic co-operation generated by geopolitical interests. He argues that:

> NATO is on solid ground as long as NATO nations are Western status quo powers; however, status quo powers will constantly be challenged to shape responses to risks; and NATO will prosper only if efforts are continuously made to bridge the general desire for the status quo with specific interests related to specific risks.

Hagel (2004) maintains that:

> Although the highest importance will remain for the military might, the future success of NATO will be determined by its members' ability to deepen and expand their co-operation in

the intelligence, law enforcement, economic, diplomatic, and humanitarian fields; and this will require adapting a new NATO strategic doctrine to fit these aims.

The outcome of the coming summits, as well as the next strategic doctrine will determine whether or not the aforementioned views were correct in their predictions about the future of the most successful Alliance in history.

CHAPTER FIVE

CONCLUSION

The concluding remarks of the previous analytical review can be encapsulated in the following points:

1- Given the fact that the Alliance is of greatest importance to 'the American empire' at least because it is the clearest embodiment of its leadership and influence on the European continent as well as worldwide, it is unlikely that the opposing forces will succeed in dragging the Alliance off course. Some American studies have suggested that no country or coalition of countries will be able to compete or share with the United States its unique status in the first half of this century. Logically, it is too difficult to assess the correctness or impartiality of these studies. However, it may be expected that, if this is the case, NATO will continue playing its role for some time to come, at least for the next 10 to 20 years, or till such a time as 'the American empire' decays, as have all other empires throughout history. Indicatively, the heads of state and governments declared at the Riga Summit, November 2006, that:

> We have today endorsed our Comprehensive Political Guidance which provides a framework and political direction for NATO's

continuing transformation, setting out, for the next 10-15 years, the priorities for all Alliance capability issues, planning disciplines and intelligence.

This seems to give some kind of assurance to the advocates of NATO's continuity and vitality, at least with regard to the first two or three decades of the twenty first century.

As far as the current relations between the allies are concerned, the European allies can only distance NATO from being entangled in such actions that are not in accordance with their perception of international legitimacy. To put it bluntly, the European allies do not usually seek to challenge US leadership, at least not to that brink of confrontation. Motkova and Korba (2004) identify three approaches in NATO towards US unipolarity: bandwagoning (UK), bonding (Letter of Eight, CEE countries) and counter-balancing (France and Germany). It is still too difficult claim that the 'counter-balancing 'approach will yield any considerable results in the coming years.

2-The maximization of the Alliance's strength, through the huge transformation process, makes it possible to ensure that the Alliance will definitely assume an international role worldwide that exceeds the limits of its geographical area. In practice, NATO performs important functions that no other institution or ad- hoc coalition is currently capable of taking over; and this will put pressure on the United States to do its best to sustain and revive the Alliance. Although the current period has shown that the United States is relying increasingly on ad hoc military coalitions, it will, predictably, come to recognize, that this policy has its faults since such arrangements tend to be fragile and unreliable because of a lack of common unifying threat or short-sighted interests.

3- While NATO is forging ever closer relations with different entities and regions worldwide, such as Russia, Ukraine, the Mediterranean and Central Asia; the EU's foreign policy is still somehow limited. In other words, EU member states have not formulated well-defined policies to deal, for example, with Central Asia or Caucasus and the Middle East. So, the leverage which these countries have enjoyed through the Alliance's mechanisms, with regard to formulating policies towards other regions, will convince them to exclude any idea of the possibility of drift or separation, if desired, until the time comes when they can build up their new and independent policies in various directions.

4-It is also perceived that even taking into account internal European considerations, NATO is still the preferable choice. Andrews (2005:29) maintains that 'most European countries in NATO and in the EU still want a firm link to the United States', whilst Laos (2000) underlines that NATO provides the most reliable guarantee of the deterrence of aggression, warning that:

> If Germany and Russia become tempted to aggression and pursue a condominium over Central Europe or quarrel with each other, then the United Kingdom and France would be unable to sustain the political balance in Western Europe without the US.

To elaborate, as the American role has been the most influential factor in achieving and completing the process of ending the artificial division of Europe, i.e. the Alliance's enlargement eastward, and securing Russia's acquiescence to this policy, it is not expected that the European allies could take, at least in the foreseeable future, the risk of losing or lessening the weight of this influence. Fear of Russia, now and in the near future, could serve as a NATO unifier. Additionally, for budgetary and electoral considerations, it seems that the European allies will continue to see the Alliance as the preferable option, at least in the foreseeable future. What is more, the member states of the North Atlantic Alliance have learnt from the experience in the Balkans and other hot areas on the European continent, that diplomacy, consultation, and engagement can work as a means of curtailing or defusing problems if supported by the strong threat of the use of force. That is why, the allies will not, most probably, at least in the short and medium terms, seek to dismantle the Alliance because this would mean denying themselves a useful tool. Moreover, NATO has a symbolic function. It represents the powerful face of the superiority of Western civilization vis à vis other civilizations. Therefore, many Westerners would prefer to keep it alive, under any circumstances, even if it shows itself unable to perform tasks to crystallize this eminence. The proof of the truth of this argument is that no country has ever tried to move out of the Alliance by terminating its membership in accordance with Article 13 of the founding Washington Treaty, in spite of any disagreements.

5- The Alliance has identified terrorism and the threat from weapons of mass destruction, as its new raison d'être for the twenty first century, after almost a decade of confused vision. The inability to deter a potential attacker, the immediacy of today's threats and the magnitude of potential harm that could be caused by the adversaries' choice of weapons, are reason enough for the parties concerned not to sever the existing ties, which provide them with the best available means of protection. The events of 11 September, 2001 were an massive and unforgettable 'cultural' shock which awoke every Western country to the reality that no country is immune any more. It goes without saying that these worries and fears were ignited and intensified by the Madrid, Istanbul, and London explosions. The effects of these waves of 'culture shock' may last for decades and generations. Coupled with this, the existing trend of maximizing NATO's role in combating terrorism, which forms part of its comprehensive new strategy, may rule out or at least weaken the arguments of those who are still casting doubts on the necessity of an Alliance. Irrefutably, NATO's existence, as such, serves certain psychological functions, and this matter has been reflected and mirrored in its new roles in securing public events, such as the Olympics in Athens and the Pope's funeral in Rome.

6-The disagreements that may occasionally occur between the allies over the appropriate measures which should be taken in relation to certain issues or countries, should not obscure the fact that the allies in general agree on many other things among which is that the Alliance is the organization most capable of dealing with the dangers that may emanate from beyond the Euro-Atlantic area, at least in the coming period; and these dangers are too big to be faced by only one pillar of the Alliance in the absence of the other pillar. To make it clearer, the current global governing rules suggest that the powerful nations tend to co-operate, not to confront each other in addressing the problem of 'others'. Whiteneck (2004) argues that:

> A global system that exhibits greater co-operation among its leading nations, with declining chances for major global conflicts and increasing coordination of complex economic and political solutions to international problems, will probably still have a number of small regional or civil conflicts and a number of nations in economic distress; but, these conflicts and the existence of economic and social distress will not be at a level of intensity that threatens systemic disruption.

7- The Alliance should no longer be perceived as a purely defensive organization which is confined to a limited geographical area, as it has been recently given a dual mandate, i.e. defensive and offensive tasks. This can be understood in the light of NATO's new military concept for defence against terrorism, which underlines the Alliance's readiness:

To act against terrorist attacks, or the threat of such attacks, directed from abroad against our populations, territory, infra-structure and forces; to provide assistance to national authorities in dealing with the consequences of terrorist attacks; to support operations by the European Union or other international orga-nizations or coalitions involving allies; and to deploy forces as and where required to carry out such missions.

Suffice it to refer to the right to act against the 'threat of such attacks' and 'directed from abroad', which can be interpreted in different manners, according to security considerations at a particular time.

It is worth indicating that the Alliance has declared that:

Military transformation is a long-term endeavor that must continue if NATO is to be able to carry out the full range of its missions including combating the threats posed by terrorism, failed states, and the proliferation of weapons of mass destruc-tion.

Noting the word 'combating' and the sources of dangers mentioned, this may amount to a clear statement that the allies, at least the majority of them, intend to make their Alliance, perhaps in the long run, the policeman of the world, even if they don't wish to declare that to public opinion. In the meantime, there is also the implication that in future cases, NATO would not need a UN mandate to operate beyond its borders; as Kosovo has set a precedent. This, certainly, reflects some concurrence with the orientations of the 'American empire' in the twenty-first century.

8- NATO is facing a number of challenges. For instance, will increasing European power, following the admission of new members, counterbalance or become equal to the American weight in the Alliance or only contribute more in weakening the role of the old Europe, meaning the Franco-German axis, etc., in favour of the United States and its European friends? So far, the new European members have shown evident support for American policy in general, perhaps to counter balance the influence of the major European states. This is likely to mean that the Alliance will be more prone toward applying coercive measures in the coming period. For the time being, the seemingly desirable options for those concerned is to find a formula that can satisfy all parties in order to avoid any risk of confrontation or exclusion. Tanugi (2003:128) underlines the importance of complementarities between a stronger Europe and a more open America, indicating that 'Europeans could help Americans share that conclusion by rejecting the choice between Europe as a power potentially antagonistic toward the United States and no Europe at all.' Monaco and Riggle (2002) stress that:

> In the post Cold War era, the brutal reality is that Europe is getting stronger every day, and is needing the United States less and less; therefore, the traditional Cold War cohesion that lined up European support automatically behind their superpower friend no longer exists, or rather, it exists in a new form.......
> There is a significant transatlantic convergence of goals and ideals, which certainly binds the partners together, but in an environment that allows for questioning and compromise.

Singer & Olin (2003) observe that:

> The key test in whatever NATO does is twofold: whether Europe has the political will to actually support NATO the way it

requires it, and whether America has the maturity and patience to work with others and compromise on some things.

Kaplan (2004:150) assesses that:

> The danger in the future lies less in the likelihood of an abrupt dissolution than in the possibility of NATO becoming as irrelevant as the League of Nations in 1930's, if America and Europe fail to share the responsibilities of crisis management beyond the boundaries of the Alliance.

It can be argued that a dose of realism is needed on both sides to ensure or prolong the future survival of the Alliance: the United States should allow the European allies to play a more decisive role in drawing up and implementing the Alliance's policies; whereas the European allies must bridge the gap in capabilities with the United States by increasing their budgets and roles to an extent that results in more balance in the division of labour on the Alliance's missions.

In general, the future of any alliance relies upon the will of its allies and their commitment to its duration and desire to preserve its concepts and values. Therefore, taking the available evidence into account, one can argue that the determinates of the destiny of the North Atlantic Alliance would include: the speed at which old Europe and new Europe moves to build an appropriate security and defence policy, not only for the European continent but also on an international scale; whether the United States pursues its unilateralist hegemonistic plans worldwide, something which would definitely antagonize Europe as well as other major poles of the world; whether the European allies will accept and agree upon the transformation of the Alliance in such a way that it becomes a policeman for the good of the United States, or whether the European allies strive to make the Alliance's policy consistent with international law. To put it another way, what remains to be seen is whether or not the growing European identity, if coupled with the manner in which the United States has chosen to establish its grand imperial project, will jeopardize the continuity of the Alliance in the long run. Answers to these questions must be deferred until the issuing of the new strategic doctrine.

BIBLIOGRAPHY AND REFERENCES

(1) Basic documents

A: Internet references
(I) Retrieved from April 2004 to December 2005
from the world wide web: http://www.nato.int/

1- All the speeches and Press statements of
   Secretary Generals from 1988 to 2006.

2- All the final declarations of the successive
   summits from 1988 to 2006

3- All the statements of ministerial meetings from 1988 to 2006.

4- All Basic documents such as, *Washington Treaty and
   Associated Declarations, Resolutions and Protocols* ; *Status of the
   Organization and Representation of Third States Agreements
   on Status of Forces and Military Headquarters*; *Partnership for
   Peace (PFP) and Euro-Atlantic Partnership Council (EAPC)
   Founding Documents*; *NATO Relations with Third States*, etc

5- The 1991 Strategic Concept.

6- The 1999 Strategic Concept.

7- NATO handbook

8- NATO Press releases from 1999 to 2006

9- Key facts: Topics (terrorism, Partnership, enlargement, etc).

10- All NATO publications such as (Backgrounder: Logistics support for NATO operations, Military matters: The beginnings of NATO's military structure: birth of the Alliance to the fall of the Berlin Wall; NATO-Russia News; NATO-Ukraine News; Security cooperation with the Mediterranean region and the broader Middle East; Building peace and stability in crisis regions; Briefing: NATO Military Structure ;Briefing: Weapons of mass destruction Briefing; Response to terrorism; Briefing: Helping secure Afghanistan's future Briefing: Improving capabilities to meet new threats; Combating terrorism: NATO's role, etc).

(2)- Books &Articles & lectures

A. Andrews (2005) 'toward transatlantic alliance'In Andrews, D (ed) *The Atlantic Alliance under stress US –European relations after Iraq.* (Cambridge: Cambridge University Press)pp.9-29

A.Lieven (2003) 'The pangs of disappointed love ? A divided West and its multiple peripheries', In Lieven,A & Trenin,D (ed) *Ambivalent neighbors The EU,NATO and the price of membership.* (Washington,D.C: Carnegie endowment for International peace) pp.295-312

A.Missiroli and G.Quille (2004) 'European Security in Flux', In Cameron,F (ed) *The Future of Europe Integration and Enlargement* (London, New York: Routledge and Taylor & Francis group) pp. 114-134

A.Moens (2002) 'Developing a NATO-EU security regime', In Hodge,C (ed) *NATO for a new century Atlanticism and European security.* (Westport & Connecticut & London: Praeger) pp.69-84

A.Tonelson (2001) 'NATO Burden – Sharing: Promises; Promises', In Carpenter, T (ed) *NATO Enters the 21 Century* (London, Portland: Frank Cass) pp. 29- 58.

A.Tonelson (2001) 'NATO Burden – Sharing: Promises; Promises', In Carpenter, T (ed) *NATO Enters the 21 Century* (London, Portland: Frank Cass) pp. 29- 58.

Barany, Z (2003). *The future of NATO expansion Four cases studies.(Cambridge*: Cambridge UniversityPress).

Bebler, A (ed). 1999. *The Challenge of NATO Enlargement.* (Westport, Connecticut: Praeger.)

Black,J (2000). *Russia faces NATO expansion Bearing gifts or bearing Arms.*(Lanbam& New York & oxford: Rowman & Littlefield publishers co).

Bluth,C & Kirchner, E& Sperling,J (ed) (1995). *The future of European security.* (Aldershot& Singapore& Sydney: Dartmouth).

Boot, Max (2004). *The "American empire" in the Middle East.* (Berkeley: Berkeley public policy Press).

Borawski, J & Young, T (2001). *NATO after 2000 The future of the Euro- Atlantic alliance.* (London & Westport & Connecticut: Praeger).

Borowski, J, Thomas-Durell Y.(2000*).NATO AFTER 2000: The futures of the Euro-Atlantic Alliance.(*Westport, Connecticut: Praeger).

Brenner,M (1998). *Terms of engagement the United States and the European security identity.* (Westport & Connecticut & London: Praeger).

Bronstone, A (2000) *European Security into the Twenty-First Century Beyond Traditional Theories of International Relations* (Aldershot, Burlington, Singapore, Sydney: Ashgate).

Bugajski, J & Teleki, I (2006). *America's new allies*. (Washington,D.C: CSIS).

C. David (1999) 'Will NATO live to celebrate its 100th birthday', In David, C & Levesque,J (ed) *The Future of NATO, Enlargement ; Russia, and European Security* (London, Ithaca: McGill –Queen 's UniversityPress) pp. 216-222.

C. Layne (2001) 'US Hegemony and the Perpetuation of NATO', In Carpenter,T (ed) *NATO Enters the 21 Century* (London, Portland: Frank Cass) pp.59-91.

C.lemens (1997) 'political options and obstacles', Clemens,C (ed) *NATO and the Quest for the Cold War Security* (London, New York: Macmillan Press, St, Martin's Press) pp.183-206.

C.Nolon & C.Hodge (2002) 'The healthy bones of a single Pomeranian Grenadier: the Atlantic alliance and the humanitarian principle',In Hodge,C (ed) *NATO for a new century Atlanticism and European*

Chernoff, F (1995). *After Bipolarity The vanishing threat theories of cooperation, and the future of the Atlantic alliance.*(Michigan: The Universityof Michigan Press).

Clemens,C (ed) (1997). *NATO and the quest for post cold war security.*(Hampshire & London: Macmillan Press LTD).

Coker, C (2002). Globalization and insecurity in the twenty –first century.NATO and the management of risk. (Oxford: IISS-Adelphi paper Oxford UniversityPress).

Cornish, P (1997) *Partnership in Crisis The US, Europe and the fall and Rise of NATO* (London: Royal Institute of International Affairs).

Crisen,S (ed) (2002, April 19). *NATO and Europe in the 21 th century New Roles for a changing partnership.*(East and West European studies).

Duignan, p (2000) *NATO   Its Past, Present, and Future* (Stanford, California: Hoover Institution Press).

Forster,P & Cimbala,S (2005). *The US, NATO and military burden –sharing.* (London & New York: Frank Cass).

Freedman, L (2005). The transatlantic Agenda: vision and counter-vision. Volume 47 number 4 pp 19-38 (London:IISS)

G.Auton (1998) 'The United States and an expanded NATO',In Dutkrewicz,P & Jackson,R (ed) *NATO looks East.*(Westport & Connecticut & London: Praeger)pp,177-190

Gebhard, P (1994) *The United States and European Security.. Will the Transatlantic Alliance become moribund through continued defence of Europe or became the linchpin of defence anywhere in the world*   (London: International Institute for Strategic Studies).

Gebhard, P (1994) *The United States and European Security.. Will the Transatlantic Alliance become moribund through continued defence of Europe or became the linchpin of defence anywhere in the world*   (London: International Institute for Strategic Studies).

Gheciu,A (2005). *NATO in the new Europe   The politics of international socialization after the cold war.*(Stanford & California: Stanford University Press).

Gordon,P & Shapiro, J (2004). *Allies at war   America and Europe and the crisis over Iraq.* (New York & London: McCraw-Hills books).

H.Gardner (2002) 'NATO: enlargement and geo-strategic history: alliances and the question of war and peace',In Hodge,C (ed) *NATO for a new century   Atlanticism and European security.* (Westport & Connecticut & London: Praeger) pp.23-45

Haass,R (2005). *The opportunity   America's moment to Alter history's course.* (New York: Public Affairs).

Haseler, S (2003). *Rethinking NATO: a European declaration of independence.* European Essay No.26. The Federal Trust for education and research.

Havel, V (2002). *NATO, Europe, and the security of democracy.*(Prague: Theo publishing pardubice).

Hodge, C (ed) (2002). *NATO for a new century Atlanticism and European security.* (Westport & Connecticut & London: Praeger).

Hyde-Price, A (2000) *Germany & European Order   Enlarging NATO and the EU* (Manchester, New York: Manchester UniversityPress).

Hyde-Price,A (1991). *European Security beyond the cold war   Four scenarios for the year 2010.* (London & New Delhi-New Bury Park: SAGA publications).

J. Simon & S. Kery (1999) 'The New NATO', In   Tiersky,R (ed) *Europe Today   National Politics, European Integration, and European Security*(lanbam, Boulder, New York, Oxford: Rownan & Littlefield Publishing) pp. 269-400.

K. Voigt (2004) 'Dealing with Terrorism: the EU and NATO', In Gardner,H (ed) *NATO and The European Union, New World, New Threats* (Aldersho, Durlington: Ashgate) pp. 171-180.

Kaplan, L (2004) *NATO Divided..NATO United The evolution of an Alliance* (London, Westport, Connecticut: Praeger).

L.Cehulic (2004) 'NATO –the new model of relations', In Cehulic,L (ed) *NATO and new international relations.* (Zagrab: Atlantic Council of Croatia,publishing and research Institute)pp.57-72

Lansford,T (2002). *All for one: Terrorism, NATO and the United States.*(Hampshire: Ashgate).

Lieven, A & Trenin, D (eds) (2003). *Ambivalent neighbours. The EU, NATO and the price of membership.* (Washington,D. C: Carnegie Endowment for International Peace).

M. Herpen (2004) 'Six dimensions of the growing Transatlantic Divide: are the US and Europe Definitely Driving themselves Apart', In Gardner,H (ed) *NATO and The European Union, New World, New Threats* (Aldersho, Durlington: Ashgate) pp. 198-216.

Mastny,V (2001). *Learning from the enemy   NATO as a model for the Warsaw pact.*(Zurich: Zurcher Beitrage).

McCalla, B(1996).   *"NATO's Persistence After the Cold War" International Organization* Vol. 50, Issue 3 (Summer, 1996):445-475.

Medcaef,J (2005). *NATO   a beginner 's guide.*(Oxford: one World).

Quinlan,M (2001). *European defense cooperation Asset or threat to NATO?.* (Washington, D.C: Woodrow Wilson center Press).

Rynning, S (2005). *NATO Renewed   The power and purpose of transatlantic cooperation.* (New York & Hampshire: Palgrave Macmillan).

S. larrabee (2004) 'ESDP and NATO', In Cehulic,L (ed) *NATO and new international relations.* (Zagrab: Atlantic Council of Croatia,publishing and research Institute)pp.38-56

S. Serfaty (2004) 'Thinking About and Beyond NATO', In Gardner,H (ed) *NATO and The European Union, New World, New Threats* (Aldersho, Durlington: Ashgate) pp. 79-90.

Schimmelfenning, F (2003) *The EU, NATO and the Integration of Europe Rules and Rhetoric* (Cambridge: Cambridge University Press).

Serfaty, S (ed) (2005). *Visions of the Atlantic Alliance.* (Washington,D.C: CSIS).

Shannon,V (2003). *Balancing Act US foreign policy and the Arab –Israeli conflicts.*(Oxford: Ashgate).

Simic, P (ed) (2002). *EU, NATO and southeastern Europe.* (Beograd: The Institute of international politics and economics).

Sloan, S (2003) *NATO, the European Union, and the Atlantic Community The transatlantic bargain reconsidered.* (Lanham& New York & Oxford: Rowman & Littlefield publishers,inc).

Sloan, S & Ham,P (2002) October –working paper. *What future for NATO.* (Centre for European reform).

Smith, M (2000). *NATO in the first decade after the cold war.*(Bardrecht& Boston & London: Kluwer Academic publishers).

Solomon, G (1998). *The NATO Enlargement Debate, 1990-1997.* (Westport, Connecticut:

T. Carpenter (1995) 'Conflicting Agendas and the Future of NATO', In Carpenter, T (ed) *The Future of NATO* (London: Frank Cass) pp 143-164.

T. Carpenter (2001) 'NATO's New Strategic Concept Coherent Blueprint or Conceptual Muddle', In Carpenter,T (ed) *NATO Enters the 21 Century* (London, Portland: Frank Cass) pp. 7-29.

T. Carpenter (2001) 'NATO's Prospect at the Dawn of the 21 Century', In Carpenter,T (ed) *NATO Enters the 21 Century* (London, Portland: Frank Cass) pp. 1-6

Tanugi, L (2003) *An Alliance at Risk   The United States and Europe Since September 11* (Baltimore, London: The Johns Hopkins University Press).

Taylor,C (2004) 04-60 Research paper. *NATO: the Istanbul summit.*(London: international affairs and defense section –House of Commons).

Tertrais

Thies,W (2003). *Friendly Rivals   Bargaining and burden sharing in NATO.*(London & New York: M.E Sharpe).

W. Hyland (1997) 'Is NATO Still Relevant',In Clemens,C (ed) *NATO and the Quest for the Cold War Security* (London, New York: Macmillan Press, St, Martin's Press) pp.154-161.

Wall, A (ed) (2002)Volume 78. *Legal and ethical lessons of NATO's Kosovo campaign.*(New Port & Rhode Island: International law studies U.S naval war college).

Yost, D (1999). *NATO Transformed: The Alliances New Roles in International security.* (Washington D.C. USIP Press Books)

(3) - Articles and other documents (Internet references)

Alani, M (2005). Arab perspectives on NATO. Retrieved 14 December 2005 From World Wide web: http://www.nato.int/docu/review/2005/issue4/english/summaries.html

Aliboni, R (2002). Strengthening NATO- Mediterranean relations: A transition to partnership. Retrieved 7 Mars 2006 from the World Wide Web: http://www.iai.it/pdf/mediterraneo/September_Seminar_inglese.PDF

Antonenko, O (2004). The NATO-Russia Council: Challenges and Opportunities. Retrieved 5 Mars 2005 from the World Wide Web: http://www.marshallcenter.org/site-text/lang-de/page-conf-2004-index/xdocs/conf/2004-conferences/static/xdocs/conf/2004-conferences/0409/antonenko-paper-en.pdf

AT THE ATLANTIC COUNCIL'S SALUTE TO THE NEW NATO. Retrieved 15 November 2005 from the world wide http://www.acus.org/Publications/Speeches/Robertson%20Speech%205%20May.pdf

Bakken, B(2003). NATO'S MEDITERRANEAN DIALOGUE LEARNING FROM OTHERS. Retrieved 2 Mars 2005 from the World Wide Web:http://www.ndc.nato.int/download/publications/bakken.pdf

Barnes,J & Haffe, M (2006). The Persian Gulf and the Geopolitics of oil. Survival. Retrieved 4 March 2005 From World WideWeb: http://www.iiss.org

Baytok, T (2003). Terrorism and NATO: Searching for a Mission. Retrieved 13 Mars 2005 from the World Wide Web:usconsulate-istanbul.org.tr/ reppub/bilgiconf/speakers/Taner%20Baytok.doc

Bergeron,J (2004). Transformation and the future of Berlin Plus. Retrieved 6 March 2006 From World Wide Web: http://www.rusi.org/go.php?structure ID S40757DA7

Blank, S (2002). NATO's Drive to the East. Retrieved 9 Mars 2005 from the World Wide Web:http://www.inthenationalinterest.com/Articles/Vol3Issue6/Vol3Issue6Blank.html

Boisgrollier,N (2005). The European Disunion. Survival. Retrieved 10 June 2006 From World WideWeb: http://www.iiss.org

Bugajski, J &Teleki,I (2006). America's new allies. Retrieved 18 May 2006 From World Wide Web: http://www.CSIS.Org/component/option.com

Burns, R (2003). The New NATO and the Greater Middle East. Retrieved 7 Mars 2005 from world wide web: http://www.state.gov/p/eur/rls/rm/2003/25602.htm

Burns, N (2004). NATO and the Greater Middle East. Retrieved 7 Mars 2005 From the World Wide: http://nato.usmission.gov/ambassador/2004/20040518_Brussels.htm

Cagaptay, S (2004). NATO's Transformative Powers Opportunities for the Greater Middle East. Retrieved 13 Mars 2005 From the World Wide Web http://www.nationalreview.com/comment/cagaptay200404020907.asp

Calleo, D (2004). The broken West. Survival. Retrieved 4 June 2006 From World Wide Web: http://www.iiss.org

Capar,C (1994). EUROPE AND THE MIDDLE EAST: AT THE CROSSROADS.Retrieved 12 Mars 2005 From the World Wide Web: http://www.nato.int/docu/review/1994/9405-7.htm

Chirac against NATO role (2004). Retrieved 8 Mars 2004 from the world wide web http://english.aljazeera.net/news/archive/archive?ArchiveId=4347

Chubin, S & Green, J & Larrabee,S (1999). NATO's New Strategic Concept and Peripheral Contingencies: The Middle East. Retrieved 8 Mars 2004 from the world wide web http://www.rand.org/pubs/conf_proceedings/

Clarke, R & Mccaffrey,B & Nelson, R (2004). NATO's Role in Confronting international terrorism. Retrieved 8 Mars 2005 from the world wide web http://www.acus.org/docs/0406-NATO_Role_Confronting_International_Terrorism.pdf

Commission of European communities. (2001).
COMMUNICATION FROM THE COMMISSION TO THE
EUROPEAN. PARLIAMENT AND THE COUNCIL. EU
RELATIONS WITH THE ISLAMIC REPUBLIC OF IRAN.
Retrieved 10 Mars 2005 from the world wide webhttp://ec.europa.
eu/comm/external_relations/iran/doc/com_2001_71en.pdf

Concept and Peripheral Contingencies: The Middle East.
Retrieved 7 Mars 2005 from world wide webhttp://www.
rand.org/publications/CF/CF149/CF149.pdf

Cooperation in the operational area between the EU and NATO
- reply to the annual report of the Council (2005). Retrieved
10 Mars 2005 from the world wide web assemblee-ueo.org/
en/documents/sessions_ordinaires/rpt/2005/1918.html

Daalder, I (1999). NATO in the 21 th century: What
purpose, what missions?. Retrieved 17 July 2006 From
World Wide Web: http://www.brookings.edu

Daalder, I (2004). An alliance of democracies: our way or the
highway. Retrieved 1 May 2006 From World Wide Web:
Http://www.brook.edu/views/on-ed/daalder/20041106 htm.

Daalder,I & Goldgeier,J (2006). Global NATO.
Retrieved 15 October 2006 from the World Wide
Web:www.foreignaffairs.org/20060901

Daalder,I (1999).NATO at 50: The summit & Beyond.
Retrieved 29 March 2006 From World Wide Web: http://
www.brookings.edu/comm/policybriefs/pb48.htm

Davis, I (2004). A Long Way From Consensus: Threat
Perceptions in European NATO and the Future of Missile
Defense. Retrieved 5 Mars 2005 from the World Wide
Web: www.basicint.org/nuclear/NMD/marshall.htm

Dobbins,J (2005). New directions for transatlantic
security cooperation. Retrieved 10 June 2006
From World WideWeb: http://www.iiss.org

Dombrowski,P & Payne,R (2006). The emerging consensus
for preventive war. Survival. Retrieved 1 June 2006
From World WideWeb: http://www.iiss.org

Donnelly, C (2004). Building a NATO partnership for the Greater
Middle East. Retrieved 14 December 2005 From World Wide web:
http://www.nato.int/docu/review/2004/issue1/english/art3.html

Dufourcq.J (2004). The transatlantic allergy: partnership or strategic
counterweight ?. Retrieved 2 May 2006 From World Wide Web:
Http://www.brook.edu/fp/cuse/analysis/Dufourcq20040120.htm

Edmunds, T (2006).NATO and its new members. Survival. Retrieved
3 July 2006 From World Wide Web: http://www.iiss.org

Empires in conflict: The growing rift between Europe and the
United States. (2003). Whitehall paper number 58. Retrieved
7 February 2005 From World Wide Web: http://www. rusi.
org /publications/Whitehall/ref:P40B349763f62c

ESDP developments and the Headline Goal 2010 – reply
to the annual report of the Council.(2005). Retrieved 10
Mars 2005 from the world wide web assembly-weu.org/
en/documents/sessions_ordinaires/rpt/2005/1898.html

European Defence integration. (2006) Retrieved 18 June 2006
From World Wide Web: http://www.CSIS.Org/isp/edi

Forster, A & Wallace,W (2001). What is NATO
for?. Survival. Retrieved 16 April 2006 From
World Wide Web: http://www.iiss.org

Freedman, L (2005). The Transatlantic Agenda: vision
and counter vision. Survival. Retrieved 4 June 2006
From World Wide Web: http://www.iiss.org

Garden, T (1996). Alliances & The Management of Conflict
in the 21st Century. Retrieved from the world wide
web 11 November 2005 fromhttp://www.tgarden.
demon.co.uk/writings/articles/older/artall.html

Gheciu, A (2003). Alliances, Alliance Theory and NATO. Retrieved from the world wide web 11 November 2005 from http://www.politics.ox.ac.uk/teaching/ug/readinglist/214/214-MT-w7-alliances-outline.pdf

Giegerich, B& Wallace,W (2004). Not such a soft power: the external deployment of European forces. Survival. Retrieved 4 April 2006 From World Wide Web: http://www.iiss.org

Gompert, D (2006). For a capability to protect: Mass killing, the African Union and NATO. Survival. Retrieved 2 July 2006 From World Wide Web: http://www.iiss.org

Gordon, P (2006). NATO's growing role in the Greater Middle East. Retrieved 15 July 2006 From World Wide Web: http://www.csis.org

Gordon, P (2001). NATO after 11 September. Survival. Retrieved 17 April 2006 From World Wide Web: http://www.iiss.org

Gordon, P (2002). NATO and the war on terrorism A changing Alliance. Retrieved 1 June 2006 From World Wide Web: Http://www.brookings.edu/Press/review/summer2002/gordon.htm.

Gordon, P (2006). NATO's growing role in the Greater Middle East. Retrieved 1 June 2006 From World Wide Web: Http://www.brookings.edu/views/papers/pgordon/emirates2006/htm

Haass, R (2002). Defining U.S. Foreign Policy in a Post-Post-Cold War World. Retrieved 12 Mars 2005 From the World Wide Web: http://www.state.gov/s/p/rem/9632.htm

Haass, R(2002). U.S.-Russian Relations in the Post-Post-Cold War World. Retrieved 16 Mars 2005 from world wide web: http://www.state.gov/s/p/rem/10643.htm

Hagel,C (2004). NATOs Role in Middle East Security Efforts. Retrieved 11 Mars 2005 from the World Wide Web: www.allamericanpatriots.com/m-news+article+storyid-1311.html

Hagel, C (2002). NATO's Role In Bringing Security To The Greater Middle East. Retrieved 11 November 2005 from the world wide web http://usinfo. state.gov/journals/itps/0604/ijpe/hagel.htm

Harle, P (2006). The state of EU-NATO cooperation. Retrieved 8 March 2006 From World Wide Web: http://www.cisis.org

Heisbourg, F (2001). Europe and the transformation of the world order. Retrieved 14 April 2006 From World Wide Web: http://www.iiss.org

Hillen, J (1998). The U.S. Role in Global Security. Retrieved 11 November 2005 from the world wide web http://www.ndu.edu/inss/strforum/SF134/forum134.html

HUMAN RIGHTS WATCH (2005). NATO and EU Must End Squabble over Darfur AirliftTurf Battle Delays Dispatch of African Union Troops to Protect Civilians. Retrieved 7 Mars 2005 from the World wide Webhttp://hrw.org/english/docs/2005/07/01/darfur11261.htm

Hunter, R (2004). NATO's next century. Retrieved 27 April 2006 From World Wide Web: http://www.brookings.edu/fp/cuse/analysis /index.htm

Hunter, R & Joulwan, G (2002). New Capabilities: Transforming NATO Forces. Retrieved 14 November 2005 from the world widehttp://www.acus.org/Publications/policypapers/internationalsecurity/Capabilites%20Gap%20Report.pdf

Initiative for a renewed transatlantic partnership.(2003). Retrieved 25 March 2006 From World Wide Web: http://www. Csis.org/Europe/initiative

International Terrorism. Retrieved 14 November 2005 from the world wide web: www.ict.org.il/inter_ter/frame.htm

Isakova,I (2005). ESDP after the EU constitution. Retrieved 6 March 2006 From World Wide Web: http://www. rusi.org/go.php?structure ID S40757DA7

Job, B (2001). Alliances' and Regional Security Developments: The Role of Regional Arrangements in the UN's Promotion of Peace and Stability. Retrieved 11 November 2005 from the World wide Web http://www.unu.edu/millennium/job.pdf

Jones, J (2005). NATO transformation and challenges. Retrieved 4 February 2005 From World Wide Web: http://www. rusi.org /go.php ? structure ID

Joyce, M (2005). NATO's quiet deployment. Retrieved 5 February 2006 From World Wide Web: http://www. rusi. org /publications/newsbrief/ref:p43e5b7a4de71

Joyce, M (2005). NATO's return to politics. Retrieved 5 February 2005 From World Wide Web: http:// www. rusi.org /go.php ? structure ID

Kaldor, M & Salmon,A (2006). Military Force and European Strategy. Survival. Retrieved 4 June 2006 From World WideWeb: http://www.iiss.org

Kaplan, L (2001). NATO ENLARGEMENT:THE ARTICLE 5 ANGLE. Retrieved 12 November 2005 from the world wide web http://www.acus.org/ Publications/bulletins/internationalsecurity/art5.pdf

Kay, S (2003). Beyond the Prague Summit: Remaking NATO The Transatlantic relationship: problems and prospects. Retrieved 14 December 2005 From World Wide web: www. nato.int/docu/review/2002/issue3/english/main_pr.html

Kourvetaris, G (2002). NATO's CHANGING ROLE/ MISSIONS AND PERSISTENCE IN THE POST COLD WAR ERA: THEORY AND PRACTICE. Retrieved 11 Mars 2005 from world wide web: http://www.waikato.ac.nz/ wfass/dan-zirker/IPSA-conf-02/George%20Kourvetaris/

The%20Evolving%20Role%20of%20NATO%20in%20t
he%20aftermath%20of%20the%20Cold%20War.htm

Kovanda, K (2004).NATO and the Greater Middle East.
Retrieved 11 Mars 2005 From the World Wide Web:
http://www.mzv.cz/servis/soubor.asp?id=6439

Kremer, M (2003). A European foreign and security
policy ?. Implication for transatlantic relations.
Retrieved 15 January 2006 from the World Wide Web:
http://www.boell.de/de/01_event/3185.html

Kristol,W (1997). NATO ENLARGEMENT. PROJECT
FOR NEW AMERCAIN CENTURY Retrieved Mars
9, 2005 from the World Wide Web: http://www.
newamericancentury.org/nato-19971008.htm

Kuhnhardt,L (2003). System-opening and Cooperative
Transformation of the Greater Middle East.a new trans-
Atlantic project and a joint Euro-Atlantic –Arab tests.
Retrieved 10 Mars 2005 from the world wide web zei.de/
zei_deutsch/propro_neu/fpg_zeic_eu_medi_dialog.htm

Laipson, E (2003). The future of NATO's Mediterranean
initiative. Retrieved 14 March 2005 From World Wide
Web: http://www.nato.int/med-dial/2003/0304-art.pdf

Laos, N (2000). INTERNATIONAL SECURITY IN THE POST-
COLD WAR ERA. Retrieved 16 Mars 2005 from world wide
web: http://www.mfa.gov.tr/grupa/percept/IV-4/laos.htm

Laos, N (2000). INTERNATIONAL SECURITY IN THE POST-
COLD WAR ERA. Retrieved 16 Mars 2005 from world wide
web: http://www.mfa.gov.tr/grupa/percept/IV-4/laos.htm

Lemine, M & Haless, O (2003)."Immigration: Stability
and Security in the Mediterranean". Retrieved 2 Mars
2 2005 from the World Wide Web:http://www.ndc.
nato.int/download/publications/amara.pdf

Lesser, I (2004). The United States and Euro-Mediterranean Relations: Evolving Attitudes and Strategies.Retrieved 10 Mars 2005 from the world wide web http://www.mafhoum.com/Press7/207P10.htm

Lindley,J (2006). Why America is stuck with NATO. Retrieved 2 Mars 2006 from the World Wide Web: www.europesword.org/article.aspx?ID=16c7be88

Linn,J (2004). Rebuilding transatlantic relations – It's time to repair damages bridges. Retrieved 2 May 2006 From World Wide Web: Http://www.brook.edu/jlinn

Lobjakas, A (2004). Middle East: U.S. Pushes For NATO Role In Surrounding Region. Retrieved 7 Mars 2005 from world wide web:http://www.rferl.org/featuresarticle/2004/02/c0d5294b-6d62-46ac-9f92-be3cc89c2b18.html

Lugar,R (2004). NATO and the Greater Middle East. Retrieved 9 Mars 2005 from the World Wide Web:http://www.securityconference.de/konferenzen/rede.php?menu_2004=&menu_konferenzen=&sprache=de&id=134&

Malmvig, H (2005). A new role NATO in the Middle East   Assessing possibilities and Barriers for an enhanced Mediterranean dialogue. Retrieved 6 Mars 2006 from the World Wide Web: www.diis.dk.

Manca,D (2003). Iran: a test case for EU non-proliferation policy. Retrieved 15 October 2005 from the World Wide Web: www.isis-europe.org

MARRAKCHI1, R (2002). LE MAROC ET LE DIALOGUE MEDITERRANEEN(in French)

Marshal, V & Rudolf, P (2004). Debate Should the Middle East be NATO's new central front? Retrieved 7 Mars 2005 from world wide web:http://www.nato.int/docu/review/2004/issue1/english/debate.html

Martellini, M & Redaelli,R (2003). Towards a Non discriminatory nuclear diplomacy versus Iran: some hints. Retrieved 15 January 2006 from the World Wide Web: www.globalsecurity.org/wmd/world/iran/links.htm -

Martin,K (2003).A European foreign and security policy?. Retrieved 13 Mars 2005 from the world wide Web weltpolitik. net/Sachgebiete/.../Aktuelle Literatur/Oktober 2003.html -

Masala, C (2005). Rising expectations. Retrieved 14 December 2005 From World Wide web: http://www.nato. int/docu/review/2005/issue4/english/summaries.html

Mateos, E & Pinyol, G (2003). European Perceptions of Southern Countries Security and Defence Issues. Retrieved 16 November 2005 from the world wide web http://www.euromesco.net

Miles, D (2004). NATO Expands Outreach to Mediterranean, Middle East. Retrieved 13 Mars 2005 From the World Wide Web:http://www.defenselink. mil/news/Jun2004/n06302004_200406307.html

Miller, J & Bucherl, W (2000). "Early Lessons form the Post-Cold War Era: Western Influences on Central and Eastern European Transitions." Conference summary. Retrieved 9 Mars 2005 from the World Wide Web: http://www.cap. uni-muenchen.de/download/2001/Transformation.PDF

Missiroli, A (2004). Central Europe between the EU and NATO. Retrieved 17 May 2006 From World Wide: http://jounalsonline. tandf.co.uk/(zbawvcvn2qxlgu451fgxiwza)/app/home/contribution

Monaco, A and Riggle, S (2002). NATO Squares Off with Middle East Foe Retrieved 11 November 2005 from the world wide web www.cesd.org

Monnet, P (2003). The Future of Security and Defence Alliances in Europe. Retrieved 11 November 2005 from the world wide web http://www.ndc.nato.int/download/research/avenir_en.pdf

Motková, H & Korba, M (2004). NATO BETWEEN PRAGUE AND ISTANBUL: Reviewing Progress, Assessing Prospects. Retrieved 17 November 2005 from world wide web fromhttp://fesportal.fes.de/pls/portal30/docs/FOLDER/WORLDWIDE/WESTSUEDEUROPA/PRAG-REPORT-NATO-MAI-2004.doc

NATO and EU must end squabble over Darfur Airlifts (2005). Retrieved 15 October 2005 from the World Wide Web: hrw.org/english/docs/2005/06/09/darfur11105.htm

NATO eyes role in Middle east peace efforts. Retrieved 8 Mars 2004 from the world wide web:http://www.chinadaily.com.cn/en/doc/2003-06/04/content_167759.htm

Naumann, K(2004) Implementing the European security and defense policy: A Practical Vision for Europe. Retrieved from the world wide web 13 November 2005 from http://www.acus.org/docs/0008-

Naumkin,V (2002). Europe's role in the Greater Middle East: A Russian Perspective. Retrieved 8 Mars 2005 from the world wide webhttp://www.eusec.org/naumkin.htm

Naummann, K. Implementing the European Security and Defense Policy: Retrieved 8 Mars 2005 from the world wide web http://www.acus.org/docs/0008-.pdf

Necas, P (2004) BEYOND TRADITION:NEW ALLIANCE'S STRATEGIC CONCEPTS. Retrieved 15 Mars 1 2005 from: http://www.ndc.nato.int/download/publications/monograph_21a.pdf

Niblett, R (2005). Overview of Transatlantic relations prior to president Bush's visit to Europe. Retrieved 5 March 2006 From World Wide Web: http://www. CSIS.Org.

Nolan, R (2004). NATO: A New Role in the Greater Middle East?. Retrieved 8 Mars 2004 from the world wide web: http://www.fpa.org/newsletter_info2583/newsletter_info_sub_list.htm?section=NATO%3A%20A%20new%20role%20in%20the%20Greater%20Middle%20East%3F

Non-EU European countries and European defence - reply to the annual report of the Council (2002). Retrieved 10 Mars 2005 from the world wide Web assembly-weu. itnetwork.fr/en/documents/.../rpt/2002/1779.html –

Nordam, J (1997). The Mediterranean dialogue: Dispelling misconceptions and building confidence. Retrieved 4 Mars 2005 from world wide web http://www.nato.int/docu/review/1997/9704-6.htm

Nye, J (1996). International Conflicts After the Cold War. Retrieved 11 Mars 2005 from world wide web http://www.colorado.edu/conflict/peace/example/nye4152.htm

PASICOLAN, P & Hwang, B (2002). The vital role of alliances in the war against terrorism. Retrieved 15 January 2004 from the world wide web http://www.heritage.org/research/index_bg2002.cfm

Perry, W (1996). Managing Conflict in the Post-Cold War Era. Retrieved 16 Mars 2005 from world wide web: www.colorado.edu/conflict/peace/example/perr5244.htm

Petersen, J (2003). The Marshall Legacy:The Role of the Transatlantic Community in Building Peace and Security. Retrieved 9 Mars 2005 from the World Wide Web: http://transatlantic.sais-jhu.edu/PDF/speeches/NORWEGIAN%20FOR.%20MINISTER%20SPEECH.pdf

Remarks by Secretary of State Madeleine Albright & panel discussion (1999). A new NATO for a new century. Retrieved 27 March 2006 From World Wide Web: http://www. Brookings.edu/comm./transcripts /19990406.htm

Rhodes, E (2003). The imperial logic of Bush 's liberal agenda. Survival. Retrieved 29 April 2006 From World Wide Web: http:// www.iiss.org

Sadakata, M (2003) Nation-Building and the Role of International Organizations. Retrieved 16 Mars 2005 from http:// wwwsoc.nii.ac.jp/jsil/annual_documents/2003/autumn/ houkoku-abstr/Panel%20F2%20Sadakata%20paper.pdf

Said, M (2003). A Southern perspective and assessment of NATO's Mediterranean security dialogue. Retrieved 14 March 2005 From World Wide Web: http:// www.nato.int/med-dial/2003/0304-art.pdf

Sangiovanni, M (2003). Why a common security and defence is bad for Europe. Retrieved 10 March 2006 From World Wide: http://jounrnalsonline.tandf.co.uk/ (zbawvcvn2qxlgu451fgxiwza)/app/home/contribution

Santis, N (2002). NATO's Agenda and the Mediterranean Dialogue. Retrieved 14 March 2005 From World Wide Web: http: http://www.nato.int/med-dial/2003/0304-art.pdf

Sanz,F (2003). A European perspective and assessment of NATO's Mediterranean security dialogue. Retrieved 14 March 2005 From World Wide Web: http:// www.nato.int/med-dial/2003/0304-art.pdf

Serfaty, S (1999). European common foreign: Security, and defence policies: implications for the United States and the Atlantic Alliance. Retrieved 25 March 2006 From World Wide Web: http://www. CSIS.Org.

Serfaty, S (2005). The United States, the European Union, and NATO After the cold war and beyond Iraq.Retrieved 8 March 2006 From World Wide Web: http://www.csis.org/europe

Shalamanov, V (2004). Transformation Concept in the Defense Planning Process - NATO Integration and Regional Cooperation (Bulgarian case). Retrieved 5 Mars 2005 from the World Wide

Web: http://www.marshallcenter.org/site-graphic/lang-en/page-conf-schedule-1/xdocs/conf/2004-conferences/static/xdocs/conf/2004-conferences/0402/shalamanov-paper-en.pdf

Shen, D. (2004). Can alliances combat contemporary threats ?. Retrieved 11 November 2005 from world wide web http://www.twq.com/04spring/docs/04spring_shen.pdf

Simpson, E (2004). NATO's Nuclear Weapons Policy: relationships to the 2000 and 2005 NPT. Retrieved 13 Mars 2005 from world wide web: http://www.pugwashgroup.ca/events/documents/2004/2004.02.26-Simpson.htm

Singer.P & Olin, J (2003). New thinking on transatlantic security: terrorism, NATO, and Beyond. Retrieved 1 June 2006 From World Wide Web: Http://www.brookings.edu/views/speeches/singer/20030115.htm

Smith, J (2006). Partners or Rivals ? The EU – NATO relationship. Retrieved 4 March 2005 From World WideWeb: http://www. CSIS.Org.

Solana, J (1997). The Future of NATO's Mediterranean Initiative. Retrieved 4 Mars 2005 from world wide web http://www.nato.int/docu/speech/1997/s971110a.htm

Solana, J (1997). NATO and the Mediterranean. Retrieved 4 Mars 2005 from world wide web: http://www.nato.int/docu/articles/1997/a970301b.htm

Soultan, G (2004). Southern Mediterranean Perceptions and proposals for Mediterranean Security. Retrieved 1 Mars 2005 from the world wide Web www.iai.it/pdf/mediterraneo/Tunis 03/Soltan_Tunis_03_finale.PDF

Steinberg,J (2003). An elective partnership: Salvaging transatlantic relations. Survival. Retrieved 5 June 2006 From World WideWeb: http://www.iiss.org

Talbott,S (2002). From Prague to Baghdad: NATO at Risk. Retrieved 1 May 2006 From World Wide Web: Http://www.brook.edu/views/articels ltalbott/2002novdec fa.htm

Tanner, F (2003). Security Governance. The difficult task. of security democratization in the Mediterranean. Retrieved 10 Mars 2005 from the world wide web gcsp.ch/E/.../Seminars/Security-Med/1st-meeting_Concept-Paper.pdf

Taylor, R (2002). Nato shifts focus to threat from south. Retrieved 12 Mars 2005 From the World Wide Web:http://www.guardian.co.uk/international/story/0%2C3604%2C724319%2C00.html

Tertrais, B. (2004). The Changing Nature of Military Alliances. Retrieved 11 November 2005 from the world wide web http://www.twq.com/04spring/docs/04spring tertrais.pdf

The Atlantic Council of the United States.(2002). U.S. Security Alliances for the Next Decade. The Atlantic Alliance The U.S.-Japan Alliance. Retrieved 14 November 2005 from the world wide web:http://www.acus.org/InternationalSecurity/alliances.htm

The Bureau of European and Canadian Affairs, State Department (1997). FACT SHEET: HOW NATO HAS CHANGED IN THE POST COLD WAR ERA Retrieved 14 Mars 2005 From the World Wide Web: http://www.mtholyoke.edu/acad/intrel/natousis.htm

THE CRUCIAL CHALLENGE POSED BY THE ARAB-ISRAELI CONFLICT.Retrieved 2 Mars 2005 from the World Wide Web: http://www.ndc.nato.int/download/publications/alsoud.pdf

The development of armaments policy in Europe - reply to the annual report of the Council.(2003). Retrieved 10 Mars 2005 from the world wide web assembly-weu.itnetwork.fr/en/documents/.../rpt/2003/1840.html

The Istanbul Initiative? Finding a Real Role for NATO in the Middle East and North Africa. (2004). Retrieved 8 Mars 2004 from the world wide web:http://www.rusi.org/publications/newsbrief/ref:P40D00C6409ACD/

Thomson, J (2003). US interests and the fate of the alliance. Retrieved 9 March 2006 From World Wide: http://journalsonline.andf.co.uk/(Zbawvcvn2qxlgu451fgxiwza)/app/home/contribution

Threat of WMD challenges Alliance. Retrieved 11 Mars 2005 From the World Wide Web:

Weaver, R (2001). NATO's evolving partnerships Building security through partnership.Retrieved 5 Mars 2005 from world wide web http://www.nato.int/docu/review/2001/0103-01.htm

Wesley, K& Chas, C & others (2001) Permanent Alliance? NATO's Prague Summit and Beyond. Retrieved 12 November 2005 from the world wide web: http://www.acus.org/Publications/policypapers/internationalsecurity/Permanent%20Alliance.pdf

What functions and interests has NATO served in the period since 1985? Why has NATO not collapsed?.Retrieved from the world wide web 12 November 2005 from http://www.geocities.com/CapeCanaveral/Launchpad/1350/essays/nato.html

Whiteneck,D (2004) Global Evolutions And The Role Of Nuclear Weapons: Alternative Futures For The Next Decade. Retrieved 4 Mars 2005 from the World Wide Web: http://www.cia.gov/nic/PDF_GIF_2020_Support/2004_05_25_papers/global_evolutions.pdf

Interviews:

1- Lord Robertson..former Secretary General of the North Atlantic Alliance

2- Ambassador minuto Rizzo... Deputy Secretary
General of the North Atlantic Alliance

3- Alberto Bin..The coordinator of the Med
dialogue and ICI initiatives.

Statement and news

BBC
CNN

Other work by the author

Islam and International Human rights
Publisher: The Arabic National House for
Culture & Publications, 2005. -Cairo -

This book is a part of research conducted at London Met University

To contact the author: mmkorfy@yahoo.com

The author is a diplomat and expert on this topic.

www.ingramcontent.com/pod-product-compliance
Lightning Source LLC
Chambersburg PA
CBHW020253290526
45784CB00003B/1224